169842

REMOV~
ALVERNO C~~~~~ LIBRARY

D0594649

Suburban Wildlife

An Introduction to the Common Animals
of Your Back Yard and Local Park

Richard Headstrom

Cover and interior illustrations by Jennifer Dewey

Foreword by Charles Roth,
Massachusetts Audubon Society

591.5

H433s

A SPECTRUM BOOK

Prentice-Hall, Inc., Englewood Cliffs, New Jersey 07632

Alverno College
Library Media Center
Milwaukee, Wisconsin

Library of Congress Cataloging in Publication Data
Headstrom, Richard (date)
   Suburban wildlife.
   (PHalarope books)
   "A Spectrum Book."
   Bibliography: p.
   1. Urban fauna.   I. Title.
QH541.5.C6H43   1984   591.5'268   83-24516
ISBN 0-13-859199-7
ISBN 0-13-859181-4 (pbk.)

PHalarope Books

PHalarope books are designed specifically for the amateur naturalist. These volumes represent excellence in natural history publishing. Each book in the PHalarope series is based on a nature course or program at the college or adult education level or is sponsored by a museum or nature center. Each PHalarope book reflects the author's teaching ability as well as writing ability.

This book is available at a special discount when ordered in bulk quantities. Contact Prentice-Hall, Inc., General Publishing Division, Special Sales, Englewood Cliffs, N.J. 07632.

© 1984 by Prentice-Hall, Inc., Englewood Cliffs, New Jersey 07632

A SPECTRUM BOOK

All rights reserved. No part of this book
may be reproduced in any form or by any means
without permission in writing from the publisher.
10 9 8 7 6 5 4 3 2 1
Printed in the United States of America

Editorial/production supervision by William P. O'Hearn
Book design by Joan Ann Jacobus
Manufacturing buyer: Edward J. Ellis
Cover design by Hal Siegel

ISBN 0-13-859199-7

ISBN 0-13-859181-4 {PBK.}

Prentice-Hall International, Inc., *London*
Prentice-Hall of Australia Pty. Limited, *Sydney*
Prentice-Hall Canada Inc., *Toronto*
Prentice-Hall of India Private Limited, *New Delhi*
Prentice-Hall of Japan, Inc., *Tokyo*
Prentice-Hall of Southeast Asia Pte. Ltd., *Singapore*
Whitehall Books Limited, *Wellington, New Zealand*
Editora Prentice-Hall do Brasil Ltda., *Rio de Janeiro*

To my Sweetheart

Richard Headstrom, author of the bestselling *Adventures with a Microscope* and *Adventures with a Hand-Lens,* is a former teacher and educator. He has also been a museum curator and a consultant for the nature programs of the Boy Scouts and Girl Scouts.

Contents

Foreword

In a day and age when animal species are vanishing from this planet at a rate somewhat in excess of one a day, it is somewhat comforting to know that other species are holding their own in our collective back yards and even expanding in range and numbers. By and large these are species that are adapted to the conditions created by the various activities of people as they cluster into metropolitan areas around the globe.

These are generally animals that do not need large wild areas for their survival but can exist in small patches of appropriate habitat and probably have one of the adaptations for moving about among these patches. They are the creatures of city and suburb—gray squirrels, raccoons, earthworms, ant lions, dragonflies, house sparrows, cardinals, praying mantis, opossums, snails, spiders, and a host of others.

Richard Headstrom has spent some fourscore years exploring the lives of such creatures and sharing his findings with hundreds of students and friends. In this book he collects much of this information in a form that will let him further increase that circle of friends. The reader will not only discover interesting facts about wildlife but will be encouraged to venture outside to see for himself, first hand. Although Headstrom has seen much over the years, he knows that there is much yet to be discovered about even the most common species by those who are observant.

It behooves us all to make the acquaintance of as many of our wild neighbors as possible, to appreciate their different ways of life, and to assure that they continue to have places in which to exist as our neighbors. Our lives are enriched as we gain insight into theirs. Our lives are diminished as they disappear.

Richard Headstrom has presented each creature as the star of a particular chapter, but as you add chapter after chapter to your pleasure you will begin to see that the lives of all these creatures are interconnected. They are also connected to the lives of the myriad creatures not included in the book. These interconnected lives make up the living fabric that clothes this planet and that includes us as well. Each extinction is a tear in that fabric. Some of the tears are minor and can be repaired; others are major. Most of the animals of this book represent the strong threads and even some patches over old tears. The fact that most of them are relatively abundant at the moment should not obscure the fact that some are not and are slowly declining. Without affection, concern, and care on our part, they could become only a fading memory.

It would be a shame if these observations of a lifetime were to end up as a requiem for a species at some future date. If, however, you enjoy this book—if you go to the field and explore for yourself and lend your voice to those who would see that we meet our human needs without losing healthy environments—then all will have profited.

Charles E. Roth
Chief of Interpretive Services
Massachusetts Audubon Society

Introduction

Few of us know much about the animals that live all around us, in the nearby field and meadow, in the nearest woods, in the not-too-distant pond or stream, along the roadside, and even in our own back yard and garden.

I have spent a lifetime studying all these animals, in the field and in the laboratory and also in my own home, having kept many of them as pets. So now I'd like to invite you to come along on a suburban nature walk with me, to see how many of the animals we might find by venturing outdoors and strolling down a roadside, following a woodland path, walking about in a field or meadow, visiting a pond or stream. As a matter of fact, we need go no farther than our own back yard or garden, where, surprisingly, we may find many of them at some time or other.

In these chapters appear, for the most part, animals that are unique in some way—they have some peculiar structure, or their bodies are modified, the better to fit them to their habitat, or they have rather odd or unusual habits or a form of behavior enabling them to more successfully meet the competition for survival. Thus, this book tells of the ingenious trap that the ant lion makes with which to capture its prey; of the stone house in which the garden snail lives and that it carries with it wherever it goes; how the water skaters skim over the surface of the water without drowning; how the sexes of the fireflies find each other by giving off light signals; of a little frog that performs acrobatic stunts; of the spiders that balloon in the air; of the lowly earthworm that is the farmer's best friend; of the hog-nosed snake that puts on an act when alarmed; how the butterflies can be identified at a distance by their individual flight patterns; how the whirligig beetles can swim around like whirling dervishes without bumping into each other; how the head and bill of the woodpecker are so constructed as to permit the bird to drill into the wood of trees without injury; how the spiders spin their eye-catching webs; how a tiny wasp fashions a jug that may well be the envy of the professional potter. These are only a few of the many wildlife facts that have intrigued me for years and may be equally fascinating to you. Best of all, to make these discoveries, you need not go on a safari to Africa nor even to a wildlife preserve. You need only venture out to your local suburban park or your own back yard to observe many of the animals that share our planet.

Common Tree Frog
The acrobat

Unlike the well-behaved child, who is seen but not heard, the common tree frog is heard but not seen. His long, reedy tremolo, which suggests the call of the red-bellied or red-headed woodpecker, is a familiar sound in our gardens on summer nights, but he remains invisible. If you try to pinpoint the song, you are likely to find it coming from a tree, a bush, or a vine, but if you look for him, the probabilities are against your finding him, for he is an elusive little animal and has the uncanny ability to make himself almost invisible.

Even during the daytime, he is rarely seen and then usually only by accident or chance. The reason for this is that he invariably harmonizes with his surroundings and can easily pass himself off as a green leaf or plant stem or as a small excrescence on the gray trunk of a birch or lichen-covered oak and thus escape detection by the keenest eye.

The common tree frog has a rather extensive wardrobe and can change his suits almost at will. In this respect he resembles the chameleon, famous for its color changes, but unlike the chameleon, whose color changes are in part due to emotional stresses or mental moods, those of the tree frog are wholly determined by environmental conditions. He usually wears a bright gray suit with dark markings (the most conspicuous of these markings being two bands on each leg and on each arm and an irregular star on the upper part of his back), but in a bright light and a high temperature he will put on a yellowish-white suit without markings.

In a dark, moist, or cool place, the tree frog seems to prefer a suit of deep stone gray or brown, and where his surroundings are green his favorite suit is one of white and green. These suits, however, are by no means the limit of his wardrobe, for he has a change of dress ranging in color from white to stone gray or brown, and from white to green, and representing all the gradations between these colors.

Like a well-dressed gentleman, the tree frog takes his time in changing his suits, usually requiring an hour or so to make any radical change in his appearance. But when he has effected a change of dress it is usually true that he then blends so well with his surroundings that he becomes as invisible as Perseus in his charmed helmet.

The tree frog makes his appearance in our gardens in early summer and often takes up his residence in some tree, where he might remain for weeks and even months at a time, as the tree provides him with everything he needs—food, shelter, and moisture. He is usually quiet during the day, but as the sun begins to sink in the western sky, he becomes restless and alert for some caterpillar, beetle, fly, aphid, or tree cricket, which he greedily snatches up with his sticky tongue. He can see moving objects at a distance of two feet or more and will unhesitatingly leap through the air after a mosquito or fly, apparently quite indifferent as to where he is going to land.

The tree frog, you see, is an acrobat without compare. Like "The Man on the Flying Trapeze,"* he will leap from branch to branch "with the greatest of ease." I have often seen one of these acrobats of the frog world leap for some slender plant stem, catch it with one hand,

---

*A popular song of some years back.

and swing in the air with outstretched legs. Then, when it seems as if he can hold on no longer, he pulls himself up to the swaying support, blinks his eyes, and settles himself comfortably as if it were all in the day's work.

I have never seen one fall very far, though I will admit my heart has skipped a beat or two on seeing one of these frogs leap through the air with seemingly no place to land. But they always find something to arrest their fall although it generally means a frantic bit of acrobatics. The tree frog is well equipped for such feats, being provided with discs on his fingers and toes that secrete a sticky substance that enables him to cling to vertical surfaces as smooth as glass. In the twilight of a summer's evening, I have frequently seen one of these frogs land on a windowpane, where it would invariably remain until night had fallen and then leave to go in search of food.

To look at a tree frog we would not believe that he is an acrobat, for his body is squat and fat with a rough, warty or granular skin that appears to be too large for the little animal, in all respects clumsy looking. But, to use an old cliché, appearances are often deceiving. His eyes are large and set in a broad and blunt head, but his ears are small—we might almost say inconspicuous—and yet they provide us with one means of distinguishing the sexes, those of the female being the smaller. Another distinguishing feature is the black throat of the male, but except for these differences the sexes are much alike both in size and color. These sexual differences do not seem to amount to much and are of value only when two specimens of opposite sex are compared.

The common tree frog disappears from our gardens and orchards sometime in September (depending on where we live), when the autumn chill warns that cold weather is on its way, and seeks some cosy cavity in a tree trunk or a hollow among the tree roots. In such a refuge, protected against the whirling snow and low temperatures of winter, he remains until the marsh marigold is once again in blossom, which is sometime in April. He then emerges and makes his way to some nearby breeding pond, as do countless others of his kind. By May numbers of the common tree frog may be observed joyously paddling about in the shallow, sun-warmed water, their high, resonant voices raised in full chorus. We might, late in the evening, find them without much difficulty, for the gnomelike males sitting on the lily pads will go on singing in the full glare of a flashlight, their vocal sacs so distended or swollen that it would seem as if they would balloon right up into the air. If you have never seen the tree frogs in the spring pond at night, be sure to do so; it is an adventure that will remain in your memory for a long time.

The tree frogs mate at night, and by the first of June they begin to lay their eggs, which are attached in small groups to plant stems, always at or near the surface of the water. The eggs, which are brown, green, or yellow in color, are laid in small masses or packets of not more than thirty or forty, though sometimes they may be deposited singly. The eggs, incidentally, are not easily found unless the grasses or other plants on which they are laid are separated or otherwise examined minutely.

The eggs hatch in from two to five days, and the tadpoles that emerge are about a quarter of an inch long and light yellow in color. They grow very quickly, in about three weeks they are not only fully formed but are also beginning to show the buds of the hind legs. Of a brilliant metallic sheen, with much gold in the skin and with a scarlet or orange vermilion tail, they are most attractive little creatures. The tadpoles are quite timid and swim about with the speed of young fish, which doubtless enables them to elude the clutches of a diving beetle or some other predator.

Some seven weeks after the eggs were laid, or about the beginning of July, the tadpoles have completed their metamorphosis and are ready to leave the water. At this time the young frogs are about half an inch in length. They begin their lives on land in a green suit, though they may soon change to a gray one or one combining these colors. They feed on spiders, flies, and plant lice. By the time they are ready to seek their winter quarters they measure about an inch in length. Meanwhile the adult frogs, after mating, have left the pond and have taken up their summer residence in some orchard, woodland, or garden, where they are likely to remain until they feel the urge to seek a place in which to spend the winter.

Chipmunk
The imp on the stone wall

One summer's day when I happened to be walking along a country road, I suddenly saw a movement out of the corner of my eye, and turning quickly, I saw a chipmunk on the stone wall that lined the road watching me with suspicion and perhaps with some apprehension, too. I looked at him and he looked at me, and for several moments we stood staring at each other, neither of us caring to make a move. At length, with what I thought was a twinkle in his eye he suddenly scampered off and was lost in the underbrush.

The chipmunk has been called the fairy of the mammal world. Webster defines a fairy as an imaginary or supernatural being or spirit, but there isn't anything imaginary or supernatural about the chipmunk; on the contrary, he is an active and alert little animal, with a saucy disposition and a mischievous twinkle in his eye. Yet I can see why, with their bright coloring, airy grace, and birdlike vivacity, chipmunks should be likened to fairies as we popularly conceive of these imaginary folk. I do not know of any inhabitant of our fields and woods so appealing as the chipmunk or so delightful to watch as he scampers merrily about or pays a hurried visit to our garden. What is more, I know of no wild animal that is such cheery company, once you make his acquaintance.

The chipmunk delights in the open woods and rocky pastures where stone walls, half-rotted logs, and thick underbrush offer safe retreat on the approach of an enemy. It is in such places that you will find him abroad during the daylight hours, for he loves the sunshine. At the very moment of writing, this elfin creature is scampering about just outside my window. Now he has climbed up on a log, and his alert, inquistive eyes scan his surroundings. The chipmunk is an extremely wary and timid animal—if alarmed, he will dash away immediately among the rocks or otherwise disappear from view, his tail held nearly erect and sometimes quivering excitedly. He has, however, a great deal of curiosity; if disturbed by the appearance of anything unusual, he will seek some safe vantage point from which to peer at it with every sign of interest and sometimes will chatter away at it after the manner of the red squirrel.

In late summer and early fall, the chipmunk is busy gathering nuts, seeds, and other edibles, which he carries in his cheek pouches and stores in the underground granary connected to his burrow. When he fills his cheeks to capacity—he has been known to carry as many as four hickory nuts at once—he looks as if he has a very bad case of the mumps.

Because of his foresight in laying up provisions, the chipmunk has been given the name of Tamias, which means "the steward." Just what purpose this reserve food serves I do not know. The chipmunk is not particularly fat when he goes into hibernation, so some naturalists seem to think that he eats some of this food before he goes to sleep for the winter, leaving the remainder for a spring breakfast; others are of the opinion that he makes use of it during the long winter months underground. Whichever the reason, he certainly stores up an abundant food supply, for as much as half a bushel or more of seeds, nuts, and other edibles has been taken from a single chamber.

The chipmunk's burrow is a rather long and complicated affair. Unlike the woodchuck, who advertises the location of his home by a conspicuous mound of earth about the entrance, the chipmunk takes every precaution to keep the location of his home a secret, as you would discover for yourself should you succeed in following him home. In digging his burrow, the chipmunk first of all chooses some likely looking spot and then excavates a perpendicular shaft several feet deep. When satisfied that he has gone deep enough, he then digs horizontally until he has excavated a burrow several yards long. Along this torturous burrow he hollows out one or more chambers up to a foot long, one of which he later carpets with grass to serve as his nest.

When he has finally completed his burrow, he makes at least two exits in inconspicuous places, such as under the edge of a stone or under the stump of a tree root. Of these two exits one is to serve as the entrance and the other as an exit should some unwanted visitor enter his home. As for the original entrance, he plugs up this hole with some of the excavated earth and smooths it over, the ground litter of leaves and the growth of plants helping to conceal it. Just what the chipmunk does with all of the excavated earth is something of a mystery. That he carries it off and scatters it is very probable, but just how he does it is a disputed point. Some naturalists think that the cheek pouches are used only to carry food, others believe that they are also used to carry the earth. At any rate, to carry all the excavated earth in his forepaws would require considerable time, and I cannot see the chipmunk engaging in such labor.

The time when the chipmunk retires to his underground home for the winter depends upon the latitude and the temperature. The average time would be from September to October, although I have seen chipmunks up and around as late as December. Anyway, in the cooler regions the chipmunk goes into hibernation when the cold weather sets in and spends the winter in more or less a state of dormancy, curled up in a ball in his underground nest.

For such an active, sun-loving animal, the first few weeks of confinement underground must be a harrowing experience. We can well imagine how it must feel to leave the bright September or October sunshine and descend into a narrow, winding tunnel, where we grope about in the dark perhaps dimly aware that we must remain there for weeks to come. Meanwhile in our cramped quarters we feel ourselves becoming drowsier and drowsier until at last we lose consciousness altogether.

The chipmunk awakes from his long winter's sleep about the middle of March, depending on locality. The warm spring sun, with the promise of many pleasant days of adventuring and chipmunk activity, entices him forth, and full of joy to be released from his underground confinement, he mounts a log or tree root and starts a loud chirpy "chuck-chuck-chuck." Other chipmunks, deep in their burrows, hear the clarion call and with a rush scamper out and add their loud and vigorous notes in a spring salute.

Chipmunks are sociable and talkative little animals, and wherever they are abundant it is not unusual to hear an animated conversation coming from some woodlot on a quiet summer's day. There may be half a dozen or more, each seated on his own particular stump or rock and exchanging chirrup for chirrup with varying inflections. This may continue for hours at a time. Occasionally they may all join in a chorus or a chant that is pleasing to the ear, but then suddenly an observer might be startled by a shrill, chirping whistle. The lively chatter has ceased as the chipmunks, seeking safety, give warning of the presence of an enemy.

The chipmunk responds quickly to overtures of friendship and becomes quite tame when he senses that no harm will befall him. He can become quite confiding and will take peanuts or other delicacies, that are held out to him. There was a time when I had a daily visitor to my garden and I always had some tidbit for him. Sometimes if I was not in the garden when he put in an appearance for his usual handout, he would climb up the screening of the porch and scratch and claw and set up an ungodly clamor until I answered his summons.

Garden Snail
The dweller in a stone house

In these days of a housing shortage, we might well look with envy upon the snails, which have no such problem. These animals build their own houses of materials that are readily available and do not cost them anything. And what is more, they carry their houses with them wherever they go. In contrast, we must stay put, and if we should suddenly take a dislike to our dwelling or neighborhood, there is very little we can do about it except to move, and that is not always possible. Snails need only go somewhere else, taking their houses with them, should they find their neighborhood suddenly intolerable.

We often speak sneeringly of a "snail's pace" when we are describing someone who is slow of movement. Yet if we had to carry a house around with us it is doubtful if we could move as fast, let alone move at all. Moreover, if we had but one foot, as the snails have, it would be inconceivable that we should even think of trying to move. It is remarkable, when we stop to think of it, how well they can get around considering their means of locomotion and what they have to carry with them. But actually a snail's foot, which is the entire lower side of the body, is one of the most wonderful means of locomotion ever devised by nature.

If you are inclined to question this, find a snail—the common garden snail is quite abundant and you should have no trouble in finding one—and place it in a glass tumbler. Then watch the snail as it climbs up the side. Observe how the foot stretches out and holds on to the glass surface. It has flanges along the sides that secrete an adhesive substance that enables the animal to cling to any surface and also has the power of letting go at will. At the same time a slime gland at the forward end of the foot deposits a film of mucus on whatever the snail moves on, movement being effected by wavelike contractions of the foot muscles, so that it lays down a sidewalk, as it were, ahead of itself on which it travels and which is always the same whether the path is rough or smooth, uphill or downhill. And should you place the snail on the ground or on a smooth surface and time its pace, you will find that the pace is always the same. It may be 2 inches per minute, 10 feet per hour, or 240 feet per day, provided the animal keeps going continuously.

As we watch a snail crawl over some surface, weighed down as it is by an unbalanced shell, for that is what the house actually is, we cannot help but marvel how the forward motion of the animal can seem to be so unconnected with an apparent muscular effort. It seems, as someone once remarked, that the slow, even progress is as mysterious and as inevitable as the march of fate.

I have yet to see an acrobat, or anyone else for that matter, as loose-jointed as a snail. When this little animal wishes to retire within its home, it merely holds its foot lengthwise and then gradually draws it within the shell. The end on which the head is located disappears first and the tail end last. Conversely, when the snail wishes to emerge, the tail end comes out first and the head end last.

The horns, of course, are not horns at all but stalks or tentacles bearing round knoblike tips. These are the eyes with which the animal can observe its surroundings. Below the stalked eyes is another pair of shorter knobbed tentacles, which are feelers, the knobs probably being organs of touch. Both the eyes and feelers can be withdrawn if the animal is alarmed or disturbed in any way.

It is amusing to watch a snail use its eyes—it often extends one eye over the edge of a leaf to see what is beyond. Sometimes the eye when so extended strikes an object. Then it is immediately pulled in and the other extended in its place but in a different direction. It is really amazing how far a snail can extend its eyes if need be.

With these two pairs of sense organs extended before it, the snail is well equipped to observe the nature of its immediate surroundings. It is said that snails can locate food that is hidden as far away as twenty inches. I have never tested them in this respect, but using a magnifying glass or hand lens, I have often watched them eat. The mouth is directly below the tentacles and is provided with one or more chitinous jaws and a long ribbonlike tongue whose outer surface is covered with rows of horny teeth. Those teeth can do a far more businesslike job than anyone would suspect.

The garden snail is primarily a herbivorous animal and obtains its food by scraping fresh or decayed leaves with its tongue. The table manners of the snail are deplorable. Give a snail an apple and you will find that it will soon make a fair-sized hole in it, but you will also find that the creature is a hopeless slobberer.

Should you examine a snail with a magnifying glass, you will see that its skin is like that of the alligator, being rough and divided into plates and with a surface like pebbled leather. You will also see a small opening on the right side where the fleshy body joins the shell. This is the breathing pore and may be seen to open and close slowly. By this motion air is sucked in and expelled, a process similar to our own breathing, although obviously much more primitive. Yet no one can deny that it is effective.

Snails are hermaphrodites. That is, they are both male and female. And yet it takes two of them to mate, which usually occurs after a more or less elaborate courtship. As far as is known, the eggs are laid in June or July, although in some cases egg laying is delayed until fall.

The eggs—fifty or more—are white and smaller than peas and are deposited under stones or decaying leaves or in shallow pits that the snails dig in the ground. When the eggs hatch, the baby snails have a shell with but one spiral turn. As the snails grow they add layer after layer to the rim about the opening, or lip, as the opening is called. These layers can be seen as ridges, and if we open an empty shell we will see the amount of growth in the size of the spirals.

The common garden snail, as well as other land snails—and there are a number of them—lives in damp places, on rotting wood, and among the fallen leaves in our gardens. Snails form their shells from the lime (calcium carbonate) that they obtain from their food and water and so must live where there is an abundance of this substance. Their shells protect them not only from injury and from various enemies but also from drying up. During dry weather they retire as far back as possible into their shells and then secrete a parchmentlike wall of mucus, called the epiphragm, across the opening. This prevents moisture (of which the snails are largely composed) from evaporating and helps the snails survive such periods of inactivity.

Most land snails are very hardy and survive cold far below the freezing point. They are, however, dormant during the winter. As the air cools in October and November, they stop eating and begin to crawl beneath stones or into tree trunks, or they bury themselves in moss, leaves, or earth. As a rule they hibernate alone. As in dry weather, they withdraw into their shells and produce a curtain of mucus over the opening. Thus boxed in, they remain dormant from four to six months. The epiphragm may be horny and transparent or chalky and opaque. In either case, it is secreted by a gland in the foot.

Butterflies
The frail children of the air

The charm of Nature, apart from the beauty and grandeur of her handiwork, lies in her capriciousness—we never know what to expect from her. We think of butterflies as part of the summer scene, flitting lazily about in the warm sunshine

> *Seeing only what is fair,*
> *Sipping only what is sweet.*

But should we stroll in the snow-clad woods during one of our midwinter thaws we are likely to come upon a number of mourning cloaks flying from tree to tree or resting with expanded wings in some sunny spot.

Such seemingly delicate, ethereal creatures would seem to be out of place in our blizzard-swept winters and yet—well put it down to a whim of Nature. Nor should we expect the first butterfly to appear in the spring to be the small, dainty spring azure; rather it would seem more fitting that some larger and seemingly hardier butterfly would be the first to venture forth after the snows of winter have melted.

But no, and although the chill winds of March still blow over the landscape, and although the woods still remain naked and patches of snow dot the ground here and there, it is the little gossamer-winged spring azure that must be the first to venture abroad and fly about "like a violet afloat" in search of an early flower.

Dainty blue in color and measuring scarcely an inch across its outstretched wings, the spring azure is a creature of many fashions. It seems as if Nature could not make up her mind just how to dress this tiny butterfly, for over a territory ranging from Labrador to Alaska and south to the Gulf of Mexico, we find one form in one locality, a different one in another. That is as Nature probably intended it to be, a source of endless labor to those of us who would study the spring azure's protean forms, for even seasonally it differs to a marked degree.

And in passing we should also mention another early appearing butterfly, namely the tortoise shell or violet tip, which we may also see flying about in the March woods. We might also see it on a branch of the sugar maple, sipping the sweet sap from a wound possibly made by a red squirrel, the little rodent being especially fond of the sugary liquid.

As the spring sun rises higher in the sky, other butterflies appear on the scene, such as the white cabbage, the yellow sulphur, the dusky meadow browns, and the queenly swallowtails, striped and belted with gay colors. Before long they will be joined by the dappled band of fritillaries, variegated by odd dashes and spots of burnished silver, the anglewings with their peacock eyes, the banded and spotted purples, and many others with names redolent of romance and far away places: the painted lady, the red admiral, the wanderer, the gray comma, the silver-spotted hesperid, the tawny emperor, the hoary elfin.

Few of us have the interest to observe the butterflies except in a most cursory manner. But if you study them closely, you will find that some species visit flowers indiscriminately, being rather catholic in their food tastes, while others are very selective and visit the blossoms of only a few plant species, perhaps only one or two. But as butterflies are more or less intimately associated with their food plants, we look for certain species in fields, others in meadows, still others in waste places and along roadsides. Or we watch for them along the woodland border, in the woodlands, or in the marsh and swamp. There is a certain amount of overlapping, since butterflies can easily pass from one habitat to another, but usually they stay where they belong.

Butterflies also have their own distinctive habits and behavior patterns. Watch an American copper on a hot, sunny day and you will see the little butterfly dart at every passing object. Even the pearl crescent chases every shadow. Three or four buckeyes often rise into the air, where they buffet each other about, rising and falling, as they engage in their aerial pugilistics. What a contrast to the lazy, easygoing satyrs and wood nymphs, the purposeful fritillaries, the bustling skippers, the sedate monarch, the vacillating blues that never seem to be able to make up their minds what to do.

Some butterflies seem to be always hungry and perpetually on the move, flying from one blossom to another; others less greedy spend long hours sunning themselves. A few species, such as the little azure, the pearl crescent, the tiger swallowtail, and the sulphurs, are as fond of water as the sugared sweets of flowers and frequently gather at a roadside puddle, the sulphurs sometimes congregating by the hundreds. We often see them suddenly rise into the air, flutter about a bit, then settle down again.

It may surprise you to learn that some butterfly species are extremely pugnacious and will chase or drive away from their territory not only other butterflies but other insects as well and, what is even more amazing, birds, dogs, and people. Butterflies have their favorite perches, too, and their own individual resting positions, whether on a leaf, a twig, or the ground. It is apparent to the most casual observer that they also have their own flight patterns. Watch a monarch and see how effortlessly it sails through the air. Or watch a grass nymph and observe how weakly it flutters above the grasses, into which it quickly drops if frightened; or keep your eye on a skipper as it darts erratically about. Just as we may identify many birds at a distance from their manner of flight, we can do the same with the butterflies.

Probably the most familiar of our butterflies is the stately monarch, which we often see from June to October flying leisurely over the fields and meadows. It is one of the largest and most distinctive of the "frail children of the air," as the American entomologist Scudder happily called the butterflies, and may easily be recognized by the brilliant copper-red color of its wings, made even more brilliant by the black markings that outline the veins and the white dots bordering them. The monarch is famous for its migratory flights. It flies south in large flocks in the fall in the manner of the birds and returns in the spring, also like the birds. How it finds its way, and above all else, why it should migrate thousands of miles in the first place is something for us to puzzle over.

The largest and perhaps the showiest of our butterflies are the papilios, which have their hind wings prolonged into curious tail-like projections suggestive of those of the swallows; hence papilios are popularly known as the swallowtails. I might add, however, that we do have papilios without tails—Lutz* facetiously called such butterflies tuxedos—and also butterflies with tails that are not papilios.

The best known of the group is doubtless the black swallowtail, a most graceful butterfly with velvety black wings that have three rows of yellow spots across them. The female has the uncanny instinct for selecting only the members of the carrot family on which to lay her eggs, for the caterpillars, or young, will feed on no other plant. This, however, is not restricted to the female of this particular butterfly, for the females of other species have the same faculty, the female monarch, for instance, laying her eggs primarily on the milkweed plant or, more accurately, on various species of milkweeds, though sometimes on the dogbane.

Among the papilios, we find that Nature has had another of her changeable moods, for in the tiger swallowtail we have the strange phenomenon of a butterfly having two or more forms arising from the same lot of eggs. In the region north of approximately the fortieth degree latitude there is but one form of this insect—the familiar yellow-and-black-striped butterfly, which we can often see visiting the apple or lilac blossoms in May and June. South of this latitude, however, there may be two forms of the female. Some are yellow and black, while others are almost wholly black or dull brownish with the hind wings touched with lines of blue and bordered with crescents of yellow and orange.

The curious part of it all is that out of a lot of eggs laid by the female butterfly some of the eggs will develop into the usual yellow form and the rest into the black form, all the eggs being of the same sex. At one time the two forms were described as separate species, and for many years they were so considered until breeding experiments proved that they were the same species.

Among the first of the butterflies to appear in the spring, the common white butterfly, or cabbage butterfly, is of particular

*Author of the well-known *Field Guide of Insects*.

interest because it is one of the few of the many imported species of which we have been able to make a complete record of the time and place where it was introduced and of its dispersal. This insect, which had been a pest in Europe for centuries on cabbage and turnip, came to our country by way of Quebec during the Civil War and has since spread over practically all of the United States. It has become established as one of the major pests of our garden crops.

Examine several specimens of the cabbage butterfly, and you will likely find that some of them have one conspicuous black spot on the upper surface of each forewing while others have two such black spots. In many insects, the sexes may be distinguished by differences in color or in color pattern. Thus in the cabbage butterfly the male has one black spot, the female two. Such differences, known as colorational antingeny, occur among insects in general but are most conspicuous or notable among the butterflies and moths.

Cousin several times removed to the cabbage butterfly is the cloudless sulphur, the common medium-sized yellow butterfly that adds such a distinctive charm to the summer landscape, flitting about from flower to flower, or in the words of James Whitcomb Riley, rising

> *Like blooms or lorn primroses*
> > *blowing loose*
> *When summer winds arise.*

There are many references to this butterfly in the writings of the New England authors, and it was an especial favorite of James Russell Lowell, who often referred to it in passages like the following: "Those old days when the balancing of a yellow butterfly over a thistle was spiritual food and lodging for a whole forenoon."

Speaking of the thistle, one of the most successful plants in the world, being found over the entire habitable globe, brings to mind the thistle butterfly, also called the painted lady and the cosmopolite. The thistle is the food plant of this particular species, and as it crept over the earth, the butterfly followed it and as a result became the most widely distributed of all known butterflies. Hence its name of the cosmopolite.

Wood Turtle

The mushroom eater

Most of us usually associate turtles with water, and rightly so. For most of these animals water is their natural element, and therefore we expect to find them in ponds and streams but not in pastures and woodlands. Yet in late spring and summer we may come upon a turtle far from any body of water and perhaps wonder how it got there. If we are familiar with turtles and their ways and recognize it as the wood turtle, it will not seem strange at all to find it on dry land for this species, unlike most others, lives largely on land.

The wood turtle, however, is not averse to water. In autumn and early spring it frequents the vicinity of brooks, ponds, and streams as well as swamps and, being an excellent swimmer, often enters the water, where it feeds upon the regular turtle diet of small aquatic animals. The reason it may be found near water during these seasons is that it hibernates in the muddy bottoms. But as soon as the spring sun serves notice that tender leaves and berries may be had for the picking, it begins to wander through pastures, woodlands, upland fields, farmlands, and even gardens.

It is rather unusual for an animal to like mushrooms, but the wood turtle appears to have a decided preference for them. How it distinguishes the poisonous kinds from the nonpoisonous ones I do not know. Or perhaps it suffers no ill effects from eating the poisonous kinds, but on this point I am also ignorant for I have never seen it eat one of them. I have often seen the wood turtle eat wild strawberries, however. I find it amusing to see how eagerly it reaches up and claws down the plants to get the berries, which it awkwardly tears off together with the leaves.

Although the wood turtle exhibits predominantly herbivorous tendencies, it will also eat animal matter. It feeds upon aquatic animals while in the water and various insects, slugs, snails, myriapods, earthworms, and crustaceans while on land. Its eating habits may often offset whatever harm it may do to our gardens, but we should not expect too much from it. It is not likely to expend time and effort in pursuing insects and other prey when it can partake of more tempting morsels with less expenditure of energy. At any rate, I have never suffered any appreciable damage from the presence of the wood turtle in my garden, nor have I ever heard of any other gardener complain of the depredations committed by one.

Someone once remarked that the turtle is somewhat of a misanthrope, showing its distrust of man by living within a shell. Yet there is some excuse for this misanthropy if we pause to think of the creatures that roamed the earth when the turtles first made their appearance. They needed some protection against the huge monsters of early geologic times, and what could be more effective than a covering of horny plates? Apparently the turtles felt that way for they have relied upon shells as a defense against their various enemies for some 175 million years. That they did not misplace their confidence in such armor is shown by the fact that during these years whole groups of weird creatures, both small and large, have come and gone while the turtles are still carrying on and probably flourishing as much today as they did in the past.

The wood turtle is easily recognized by its carved or sculptured upper shell. Should we need added marks for identification we might note that, with the exception of the top of the head and feet, which are rusty black and brown, all of the soft parts are a salmon red. Those and the gray brown of the upper shell conceal the turtle in the background of dead grasses and fallen leaves, although it hardly needs such protection.

Protective coloration is of value to the turtlets, however, for Nature left them soft, defenseless, and perhaps too brightly ornamented. Infancy is the critical stage in the lives of all turtles, and the babies fall easy prey to most of their enemies. But to make amends for her thoughtlessness, Nature has made them masters of concealment and has granted them a remarkable independence from food. After they emerge from the eggs turtles can live for weeks or months without food.

There are doubtless inconveniences to living constantly within a bony covering, but I daresay that the turtle does not mind. It is surprising how agile and active a turtle really is despite what might seem a hindrance. Our wood turtle covers the ground easily and is no mean swimmer. It is also an astonishingly good climber. One that I know of got over the chickenwire fence of a rabbit pen, and another emerged from a wastebasket that was about thirty inches high and had bulging sides.

The wood turtle is an alert, intelligent animal and can be made to take food readily from one's hand. It will even learn to beg for food, making known its wants by waving a leg or walking around a circle a few feet in diameter. To test its intelligence, a wood turtle has been placed in a maze with a compartment containing food as a goal. In order to reach the goal three correct turns at ends of passages had to be made and one blind alley passed by. Seven runs took 15, 9, 10, 9, 6, 5.5, and 5.5 minutes with 4, 3, 3, 3, 0, 0, and 0 errors per run, respectively. As a result of the experiment the conclusion was reached that "the learning of the turtle equalled the expected accomplishment of a rat in the same maze under ordinary experimental conditions."

In the above experiment it was found that the turtle seemed to depend largely on sight in its choice of a path. At each turn it looked all about before coming to a decision as to what path to take. Other experiments have tended to show that the behavior of the wood turtle is on a par with that of various mammals which also holds true for most other species of turtles.

Turtles have well-developed middle and inner ears but cannot hear in the ordinary sense. Experiments have shown that they do respond to sound waves in the air. The matter is of more than passing interest for when courting and mating, turtles grunt and make other sounds. The male wood turtle is known to make a "distinct yet subdued note not unlike that of a teakettle," audible for thirty or forty feet. The female, too, can emit a low whistle. It has been reported that during the mating the male repeatedly whistles at the female, from which it has been concluded that the whistling has a sexual significance. The whistling, however, appears to be a by-product of courtship rather than being an overt attempt to attract the attention of a mate.

The fact that turtles make sounds presupposes that they can hear, even though they have lost the use of their ears. It seems that they use other senses as a sort of substitute, for a turtle responds to slight vibrations transmitted to the skin or shell through solids—through the ground, for instance. A turtle feels the lightest tap on its shell and will become aware of an animal or person approaching it even though vision may be cut off.

The wood turtle always mates in water and generally in May or June, though wood turtles have been observed mating in October. The female usually selects midafternoon as the time to lay her eggs and as a rule chooses a sandy site near water, although she may lay her eggs upland. In common with other turtles, she buries her eggs, which number from seven to twelve, and after covering them, leaves them to be hatched by the sun.

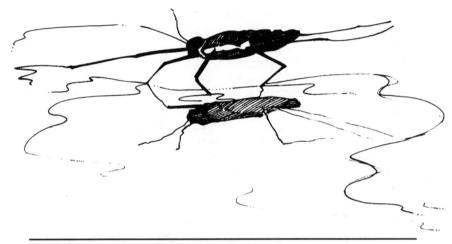

Water Striders
The water skaters

I first saw water skaters, perhaps more popularly known as water striders, a long time ago when I happened to come upon a brook that flowed through a woodland glen. They were skating about on the surface of the water. Memories can often linger through the years, and I still vividly recall that lovely spring day when I first encountered these curious, slender, long-legged insects and became insensible of time as I observed them gliding about. Even today when I am outdoors rambling about the countryside, I often stop and watch them in a running brook or in a quiet inlet of a pond. They dart here and there or drift with the current or leap up into the air and then alight on the water without breaking the surface film. All the time they create dimples that make shadows on the bottom mud and attract one's attention to the insects as much as the insects themselves.

At times they will gather in schools in some sheltered spot, as if to discuss some weighty problem or to exchange the gossip of the day, scattering for some refuge if alarmed but quickly congregating again when all danger, real or fancied, has passed.

We can understand easily enough how insects can swim on the surface of the water, but how the water striders can skate or glide over the surface without breaking the surface film is something else and might appear to be rather a mystery. But as with the illusions that professional magicians create for our entertainment, the answer is simple enough.

Capture a water strider with a kitchen sieve, a water net, or any other kind of scoop, though it will require a little patience and a certain amount of dexterity for they are extremely fast moving. Then examine it closely with a hand lens or magnifying glass and you will find that both its feet and body are covered with soft, velvetlike hairs. These hairs prevent the insect from getting wet and becoming heavy enough to sink. These hairs also envelope a silvery film of air that enables the insect to submerge occasionally and to remain for a time beneath the surface.

But the hairs are only part of the answer. Actually the reason they can skim about on the surface of the water is much the same reason that we can float a needle on water. It all has to do with surface tension.

A simple experiment will serve to illustrate this seemingly strange phenomenon. We thoroughly dry a steel needle, then hold it parallel to the surface of some water in a glass tumbler and gently lower it onto the surface so that it floats. If we look carefully we can observe how the surface film bends beneath the weight of the needle but does not break. Just how strong the surface film is can be shown by the following experiment. We bend the point end of a pin to make a hook, or we use a piece of fine wire. We sharpen the point of the hook until it is very sharp. Next we place our eye on the level with the surface of the water in the glass tumbler; then we place the hook under the surface of the water and gently raise the point to the surface. If we are careful the point will not penetrate the surface film but will lift it slightly upward.

The water striders are able to remain on the surface for the same reason. Because of their lightness and the hairs on their legs, they exert only a slight pressure on the surface film, enough to dimple it but not to break it.

In skating over the surface of the water, the water striders push themselves along with the middle pair of legs and steer with the last. They use the first pair for capturing other insects, dead or living, such as backswimmers, emerging midges that come up from the water below them, and leafhoppers that fall on the water from overhanging shrubs and other plants that line the brookside or the edge of the pond.

The water striders pass the winter beneath protecting mud banks and may often be found clustered in tangled growths of chara and elodea. On warm days they often come out for exercise. Although the young and many adults lack wings, the adults of some species have wings and can fly from one pond or stream to another. A point of interest is the fact that some species of water striders live in midocean and are the only insects that do so. It seems incredible that such fragile-appearing insects can survive the high seas of a storm, but they cling, doubtless half drowned, to some floating object or seaweed until the storm has passed and they have a chance to dry off.

Raccoon
The washer

Those of us who are hardy enough to brave the chill winds of March to tramp about the countryside are likely to find in the soggy woodland or on the muddy banks of a stream the footprints of the raccoon on a trial trip abroad. He has come out to see if the weather is such that he should remain up and about or return to his winter shelter. Anyone seeing the raccoon's prints for the first time might easily mistake them for a child's, and thus they are readily recognized. The print of the hind foot is long with a narrow and well-defined heel and five comparatively short toes; that of the front print is smaller and resembles a small hand. Normally the animal takes a stride of about seven inches and sets the hind foot in the track made by the fore foot so that only the print of the hind foot remains. But when in a hurry the animal covers the ground in a series of leaps, the prints then being anywhere up to twenty inches apart, with the prints of the hind feet being paired and those of the two fore feet being between and behind them.

We see the tracks of the raccoon more frequently in the spring, though we may also find them in the snow during the winter, for the raccoon is not a true hibernator and often appears during mild spells in December and January. Such foraging expeditions are, however, usually short-lived. With a drop of temperature he hurries back to the warmth of his retreat until the sun lures him out again.

More often than not he will go back to sleep, and as a rule it is not until spring has arrived that he will finally emerge to search for snakes and insects among the sodden leaves and debris left by the melting snows. At this time of the year food is not too plentiful and he is often compelled to go hungry although he will eat almost anything that he might find, except herbage.

As a matter of fact the raccoon does not seem to care what he eats. He is especially fond of fish and will sit on the bank of a stream and catch any fish that might come within reach by a stroke of his paw, the extended claws serving as hooks. He has also a special liking for freshwater clams and crayfish and haunts the bayous and inlets of the Gulf Coast for oysters. We might well wonder how he can open them, but with one crunch he breaks the hinge that holds the two valves together and then extracts the flesh with his paws. He is, moreover, a skillful frog catcher and goes after them both in the ponds and in the marshes. He is not averse to robbing a chicken coop either and, being a night wanderer, often surprises sleeping birds, both on the ground and among the tree branches.

In thick woods, the raccoon will frequently travel a considerable distance in the tree tops, when he will not infrequently come upon a squirrel's nest, which he will tear to pieces, compelling the terrified occupants to scatter as best they can. He has a special predilection for corn and in summer will often invade a garden, stripping the husks and in sheer wastefulness often destroying several times as much as he eats. And in common with many other mammals he feeds on countless crickets and grasshoppers and will also dig out of the ground the nests of bumblebees and hornets, his long thick fur permitting him to do so in comparative safety. But his diet does not consist wholly of animal life for he will include in his menu such diverse items as berries, grapes, nuts, and grains.

As the raccoon shows a preference for water life, he is

usually found in the vicinity of a stream, lake, or marsh. Moreover, such a location enables him to engage in his singular but commendable habit of washing his food before eating it. Sometimes he will carry this peculiar trait to an excess for he will wash a frog before eating it though it may be dripping with water from the pond or stream in which it was caught. A great many people believe that the raccoon always washes his food before eating it. That may be true in captivity but not always in the wild simply because he often finds his food in places not accessible to water.

On seeing a raccoon for the first time shuffling about in the woods in a wholly bearlike manner, we are apt to form a wrong impression about this rather heavy animal. He is actually very agile and an expert climber, using his sharp claws to ascend a tree of almost any size with an amazing celerity. He is not, however, strictly arboreal in habits, for he neither hunts his prey in the tree tops nor feeds upon the twigs and shoots. He does, however, spend as much time in the trees as he does on the ground, a hollow tree usually serving as his home although he does at times make use of a large fissure in a cliff as a den site. The trees, too, provide him with a refuge, when pursued by an enemy, he will remain in a tree until he can escape or is captured, clinging to the tree even while it is felled.

The raccoon is a night wanderer, prowling about wet places and foraging among creeks and streams. He often becomes a victim of temptation, for he delights in mounting a fallen tree and running along it, a habit made use of by hunters who set their traps on prostrate logs without the use of bait or any other inducement. With sunrise he might seek a hawk's or crow's nest in which to sleep, or he might flatten himself out along a heavy branch or perhaps climb to the topmost branches and there encircle the trunk with his body. It is rather amusing to watch him adapt his fat body to the uneven bed, doing so with apparently as much comfort as when we stretch out on a soft and downy mattress, then tucking his nose down between his paws and curling his tail about him, thus making himself a huge furry ball. It is now that the rings on his tail serve a useful purpose, for they provide him with camouflage by blending with the shadows cast by the branches in the sunlight.

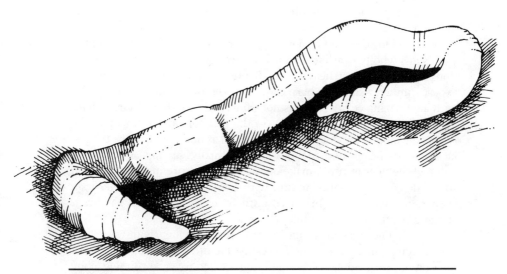

Earthworm
The silent partner

All of us are familiar with the earthworms that we find littering our sidewalks after a heavy shower and spade up when digging in our gardens. Most of us seem to think that they are of no possible use except as bait to catch fish.

But they are among the most useful of animals, as we shall see. For unseen, they work day and night, plowing, harrowing, and fertilizing the soil for our benefit.

Many years ago Charles Darwin in writing about earthworms said in his book *The Formation of Vegetable Mold Through the Action of Worms* that "it may be doubted if there are any other animals which have played such an important part in the history of the world as these lowly organized creatures." This may seem to be a rather far-reaching statement but there is nevertheless a great deal of truth in it.

The earthworm generally burrows from twelve to eighteen inches into the ground but at times may go as deep as seven or eight feet, bringing the subsoil to the surface, which is just what we do when we plow. It also grinds this soil in its gizzard and thus breaks it up as we do with our harrow, incidentally turning out a soil of much finer texture than we are able to do. And it even fertilizes the soil, for it has glands that secrete lime, which neutralizes the acids in the soil.

The earthworm, however, is not merely a tiller of the soil: It is an agriculturist as well. For it plants seeds fallen on the ground by covering them with soil that it brings up from below the surface. Then it cares for the growing plants by cultivating the soil around their roots. Moreover, it also enriches the soil by burying the bones of dead animals along with shells, leaves, twigs, and other organic matter, which upon decaying, furnish the necessary minerals to the growing plants. It even provides for drainage by boring holes to carry off the surplus water and by doing so promotes aeration. As a matter of fact, if it were not for the earthworm, vegetation would not be so luxuriant, and much of the earth's soil would be useless to many plants.

The changing character of the landscape and much of the beauty of our fields and forests can be attributed to the labors of this diminutive workman; the earthworm can also be credited with having preserved many ancient ruins and works of art by covering them with earth. The familiar mounds of black earth or castings that we often see on the ground or on our lawns are particles of soil swallowed by the earthworms in their burrows and brought to the surface. Darwin estimated that one acre of ground may contain as many as fifty thousand earthworms and that they may carry more than eighteen tons of soil to the surface in a single year, while in twenty years they may transfer a layer of soil some three inches thick. He also speaks of a stony field that was so changed after twenty years that a horse could gallop over it from one end to the other without striking a single stone.

Earthworms are strictly nocturnal animals and are not found outside their burrows during the day unless "drowned out" by a heavy rain. During the daylight hours they remain stretched out in their burrows with their heads—or rather their anterior ends, for they do not have heads in the strictest meaning of the word—near the surface. Apparently, for some reason, they cannot find their way back to their burrows if they leave them; hence they anchor themselves to the walls as they extend themselves over the surface of the ground in search of food. They eat earth, leaves, flowers, raw meat, fat, and even fellow earthworms, as they exhibit cannibalistic tendencies at times. Everyone at some time has seen a robin tugging away at a protesting worm in an effort to dislodge it; if you have ever tried it you doubtless found it was not an easy thing to do.

Run your fingers over the earthworm's body, and you will find it rough to the touch. This roughness is due to numerous tiny, bristlelike projections, or setae, which protrude from small sacs in the body wall and can be extended or retracted by special muscles. When the earthworm wants to remain fixed in its burrow, it simply extends the setae out beyond the surface of the body and into the sides of the burrow. Then it will be securely anchored or relatively so. When the animal wants to change its position, it retracts the *setae* and is then free to move. The earthworm, of course, is not so securely fixed in its burrow that it cannot be dislodged, but if dislodged it will most likely be injured or even killed.

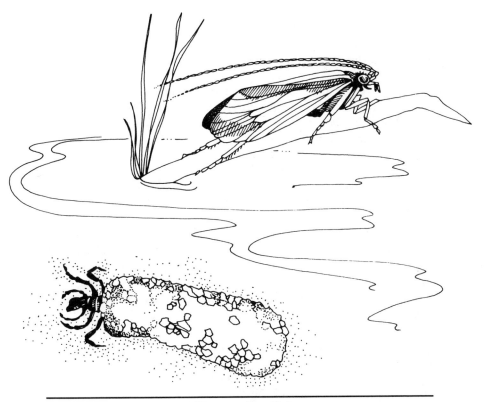

Caddisworms
The tube makers

One interesting facet of insect study is the diversity of temporary shelters that many insects build in which to pass some stage of their life cycle. I am thinking particularly of the caddisworms, which are not worms at all but the larvae or young of the caddis flies, small insects that resemble moths, though their bodies are more slender and more delicately built.

Caddisworms look like caterpillars and like them have chewing mouth parts and well-developed thoracic legs, but unlike caterpillars they have only one pair of abdominal legs or prolegs. In some species, those that build cases, there are three tubercles on the first abdominal segment, one dorsal, tubercle, and one on each side. The latter are known as spacing humps as they provide a space between the insect and its case so that water for respiration may circulate freely. We must add, however, that some caddisworms do not have these tubercles.

The caddisworms extract the oxygen from the water by means of filamentous gills, which in many species are attached along the sides of the abdomen. The water enters through the opening of the case at one end and passes out at the other, circulating over the gills by undulating movements of the insect's body.

When the caddisworms outgrow the cases, as they eventually do, they either discard them and build new ones or enlarge them by building on to the front end. When full grown and ready to pass into the stage in which they transform into adult flies—in other words when they pupate—some species cement a small stone or grains of sand over the front opening, others build a silken lid with a slit in it, and still others fashion a silken grating in each end. The object is to prevent intruders from entering the case during the pupal period. But at no time is the opening completely closed so as to exclude the water so necessary for respiration: that can still continue to flow and circulate over the gills.

The pupae of the caddis flies are as aquatic as the larvae and, like them, have gills. They are also like the larvae in being active, and in the same manner, they continue their undulating movements to keep the water flowing over the gills. Such species that live in swift water, when ready to emerge as adults, leave their cases, swim to the surface, shed their pupal skin, and fly into the air. Those that live in quiet waters merely climb out on the shore or upon some projecting stone and there shed the skin when they take to the air.

The caddisworms occur in practically every kind of aquatic situation and can be found throughout the summer; a few species, especially the net builders, may be found all winter. Look in the shallows along the edge of almost any pond or stream and you will likely observe what appear to be bits of rubbish or bundles of sand grains or pieces of leaves moving as if carried with the water currents. But remove any of them from the water and look at them closely, and you will find that they are inhabited by wormlike creatures.

Caddisworms live for the most part on vegetable matter. Most of them, but not all, construct portable cases in which they live and which they drag about with them wherever they go. Only the front end of the body and their legs project from the case as they travel, and they are ever on the alert to withdraw into their cases whenever alarmed. We may well ask at this point how the caddisworms manage to hold on to their cases as they move about. But there is no mystery about it, for the prolegs are provided with hooks, called drag hooks, which anchor the animals to their cases.

The cases of the different species differ greatly in form and in the materials used, but what is most interesting is that each species builds its own kind or style of case and uses its own specific kind of materials with which to do so. A variety of materials are used, such as particles of dead leaves, sticks, pebbles, and sand grains, all of which are cemented together with a silk secreted by modified salivary glands. The silk is not spun into a thread but is poured forth in a gluelike sheet upon the materials to be cemented together.

Fireflies
The animated lanterns

Even today, after many years of watching them, I still enjoy sitting on my porch in the twilight of a summer's evening and watching the fireflies light up the darkening scene with flashes from their lanterns.

Since time immemorial the fireflies, or lightning bugs as they are sometimes called, have excited the imagination of many peoples. Thus they are frequently featured in Japanese art and in Japan are regarded as blessed by being the ghosts of slain warriors, who have won eternal bliss by virtue of having sacrificed their lives for their country. Then they have also served as the subject of many musical and poetic compositions, some serious and some in a lighter vein.

The fireflies, which are neither flies nor on fire, are soft-bodied beetles of small or medium size. They have a prothorax (the anterior segment of the thorax) that is expanded in a thin projecting margin, which in most cases completely covers the head, and wing covers that are rather soft and strongly embrace the sides of the abdomen, as they do with most other beetles. The light that fireflies produce is not like the light produced by a burning candle, nor is it like the light emitted by an electric light bulb; on the contrary the firefly's light is the result of a chemical reaction.

The little animated lanterns make a sporadic appearance in early June, when they appear as tiny meteors shooting through the darkness, but a week or two later they are out in full force. We have all seen them, or rather their flashing beacons, for only a few of us are able to recognize them during the daylight hours.

We may well pose the question, Of what use is the light to the firefly? It is more than merely an academic question as there are many species of nonluminous fireflies that appear to survive just as well as the luminous kinds. It was believed at one time that the light serves as a warning to nocturnal birds, bats, and other insectivorous animals, a view supported by the fact that fireflies are not acceptable to the birds. But the present view is that the light is a signal to their mates, since the females of some species are wingless. Yet there are wingless females of other insects that do not need light to attract the males; nor are luminous larvae, the so-called glowworms, interested in mating. However, if the light is used to attract the mates, the supposition is that they can see each other's light.

The light given off by the fireflies is almost perfect light. In other words, the rays are almost entirely light rays, with practically no thermal or actinic rays. The firefly's light is what might be said to be cold light and is said to be between 92 and 100 percent efficient. Just what this means can be shown by the fact that the radiations of an ordinary gas flame contain less than 3 percent of visible rays, those of the electric arc only 10 percent, and those of the sun but 35 percent.

And now we may ask, How does the firefly produce its light? The firefly, like other insects, breathes by means of a network of fine air tubes that open to the exterior, these openings being located on the ventral side of the abdomen. In certain parts of the breathing system the two chemicals luciferase and luciferin are produced by certain differentiated cells, which form the light organ. The luciferase is what is known as a catalyzer, a substance that promotes or hastens a chemical reaction but otherwise takes no part in it and remains unchanged. Now when oxygen is taken into the breathing tubes it combines with luciferin without emitting light, but if the two substances are brought together in the presence of the catalyzer luciferase, which is under the control of the nervous system, they unite so rapidly that light is produced. Apparently the firefly can increase or decrease the brilliancy of the light by regulating the flow of oxygen through the air tubes, and it can display the light to best advantage by raising its wing covers during flight.

Each species of firefly has its own characteristic method of flashing, distinguishable by such features as intensity, duration, number and intervals between flashes, and flight levels. So with a little effort we can learn to identify the various species.

One of the more common species is *photuris pennsylvanicus*. The males usually occupy the tree tops and flash three, four, or five times at intervals of 2.3 seconds and with a greenish blue or pale blue light; the females remain on the ground and flash one, two, or three times during each period.

Another fairly common species is *photinus marginellus*. The males usually occupy low shrubs; the females are closer to the ground. The light of this firefly is yellow, the flash of the male being somewhat stronger than that of the female. This firefly starts flashing just as twilight ends and tends to stop when darkness has fallen completely, though stragglers may continue to flash well into the night.

A third species, *photinus pyralis*, usually begins by flying close to the ground in early evening but later flies somewhat higher, though it never attains any great height. It has a rather undulating sort of flight and always flashes as it rises in the air; then after flashing, it drops down. It has a yellow light, and when this species appears in numbers, the flashes are like brilliant sparks shooting from the ground.

Spring Peeper
The voice from the pond

We may first hear the call of the spring peeper issuing from a pond or woodland pool as early as February. Try as we may to trace the source of the call, which is much like a bird's call note, we are wasting our efforts, for at that time of the year with the ponds and pools more or less ice-bound, the peeper remains a mysterious piping voice.

And should we revisit the same pond or pool in March and scrutinize every leaf and every stick and bit of grass, or poke around among the dead leaves and mosses along the water's edge, he would probably still be elusive. As long as the air is chilly, he will remain well hidden.

But then in April, when the days have grown warmer, and

the ponds and pools have begun to teem with life, we should have better luck. For on hearing the "pee-eep, pee-eep, pee-eep" and looking in the direction whence it came, we should see a little brown body swim vigorously through the water and then climb up on a floating twig or some other support. The peeper will likely not stay there for very long but will plunge into the water and swim to the protective covering of floating leaves. There he will begin to sing, and we can see his swollen throat gleaming like a white bubble. Another peeper may join him, and a third and a fourth and still others until many have joined the chorus. But should we make some kind of a sound, ever so slight, at once there will be complete silence.

Unless the day is overcast or a light rain is falling, we are not apt to hear the little frogs until late in the day or when the sun begins to sink in the western sky. Then they begin to sing in earnest, and throughout the night their high-pitched chorus, which reminds us of sleigh bells, can be heard for half a mile or more.

When I first saw a peeper and watched him sing, I realized why he is so elusive. He is so small, measuring only about an inch long, and in color so like his surroundings, whether it is the pond or pool, lowland marsh, swamp, meadow, or woodland, that it is surprising he is ever seen. Both his markings—a V-shaped dark mark between the eyes, an oblique cross on the back, and bars on the legs—and his color—varying from a light fawn to a dark brown, the brown sometimes being yellow, red, or ashy—help in concealing him among the foliage and vegetation of his natural habitat.

The peepers begin to mate about the first of April, the males reaching the breeding ponds or pools before the females and always appearing to be the more numerous. The eggs are laid singly, never in masses, among the leaves and grasses near or on the bottom in shallow water. They number from eight hundred to one thousand and are white or creamy and black or brownish in color. The young tadpoles begin transforming and coming on land in July when they are little half-inch frogs. The adults leave the water earlier, scattering into moist, shadowy places and woodlands, where we might find them in all sorts of unexpected places—on tree trunks, in alder or huckleberry, or on tall ferns, but more usually on the ground, among the Virginia creeper or trailing partridge berry, hunting small insects. That seems to be their main interest in life. On a bright, sunny day in autumn we might hear a peeper call, giving voice perhaps for the last time before nestling down under the moss and leaves for its winter sleep.

Moths
The night flyers

All of us know the woolly bears, at least from our childhood when we used to see them in late summer or early fall crawling over the ground in what seemed to be unusual haste. And well might it have been, for they were anxious to find a snug retreat in which to spend the winter.

The woolly bears, also sometimes known as hedgehogs from their trick of curling up and lying motionless when disturbed (a habit of the hedgehog) has bands of red and black, as you may recall. The amount of black in the animal's fur varies greatly and is supposed to foretell the weather. I rather think, though, that it is a record of past weather, since the amount of black is determined by the wetness or dryness of the woolly bear's environment, moist conditions increasing the amount of black and, conversely, dry conditions increasing the amount of red.

There are other woolly bears besides the common black and red one—in fact some two thousand of them. The yellow bear of our gardens is one, and another is the gay harlequin caterpillar which we might often find on milkweed plants. I have frequently seen a number of harlequins feeding together in apparent disregard of birds. Of course, most of the birds have little taste for hairy caterpillars anyway, but the harlequins probably acquire additional protection from their food as do the milkweed or monarch caterpillars. And also like the milkweed caterpillars, their bright color scheme of black and yellow doubtless serves as a warning signal to birds. All of the woolly bears transform into small moths, some of which are exceedingly pretty. These moths taken collectively are called tiger moths, and it was these that Keats had in mind when he wrote:

> *All diamonded with panes of quaint device,*
> *Innumerable of stains, and splendid dyes,*
> *As are the Tiger Moths' deep damask wings.*

Most of us are not as familiar with the moths as with the butterflies, primarily for the reason that moths are nocturnal and are not abroad during the daytime. An exception, however, is the hummingbird moth which, when in motion or when hovering about a flower, so closely resembles the hummingbird that we are often deceived by it. This moth belongs to a group of moths all of which are exceptionally strong flyers. Linnaeus, who gave names to so many plants and animals, thought he saw a resemblance to the Egyptian sphinx in the more-or-less sphinxlike attitude of the caterpillars when at rest, and so called them the Sphinx moths. He named the family to which they all belong the Sphingidae.

The caterpillars of these moths, unlike the woolly bears, are hairless except when young and usually have a horn, which, incidentally, is harmless, at the hind end of the body. When fully grown they pupate or transform into the adult moths in or near the ground, some pupae having a "handle," which is really a sheath for the long tongue. Sometimes when spading the garden we unearth a brown, segmented shell that looks like a jug with a handle at one side. Should you ever do so, you will know that it is a sphinx pupa and probably that of the common tomato sphinx, as the caterpillars of this moth are frequently found in our gardens feeding on the tomato plants.

The sphinx moths are beautiful creatures and have a distinctly tailor-made appearance. They have long, rather pointed wings, which enable them to fly with extraordinary speed. Most of them also have remarkably long tongues, which when not in use are coiled up in front of and beneath the head like a watch spring. This adaptation permits them to gather the nectar of such flowers as the petunia, morning-glory, and nasturtium, which have their nectar wells deep within their tubular corollas.

Because of their large size, beautiful colors, and often conspicuous cocoons, the giant silkworm moths are the delight of every beginning lepidopterist. Some of the more common species are the *cecropia*, *promethea*, *polyphemus*, and *luna*, the last named generally considered to be our most beautiful insect. It is a lovely green, but unfortunately when it is pinned in an exhibition case, the green fades rapidly to a light gray.

Despite their size, the giant silkworm moths are rarely seen, as they are all night flyers. To see them we must be interested in the visitors to street and porch lights. The caterpillars, too, are rarely found, since they are protectively colored and blend with the foliage on which they feed. None of them, incidentally, occur in sufficient numbers to be injurious.

The *cecropia* moth, apparently named after Cecrops, king of Attica (but why I don't know), is the largest of these giant moths, with a wingspread up to six and a half inches. Children used to call the cocoon of this moth the cradle cocoon because it is shaped like a hammock and is suspended close beneath a branch.

Somewhat smaller but more common than the *cecropia*, the *promethea* moth appears to have been mistakenly named for Prometheus, the name of one of the Titans, all of whom were fabled to be of gigantic size. The male and female of this species are so unlike each other that they might easily be mistaken for distinct species. During the winter we may often observe dead leaves hanging from the branches of such trees as the wild cherry, sassafras, and ash. If we examine the leaves, we will most likely find each of them to be wrapped around a cocoon of this moth. Sometimes there may be so many of these cocoons on a tree as to be a prominent feature of the winter landscape.

Like the cocoons of the *promethea* moth, those of the *polyphemus* moth are also enclosed within leaves, but they are not quite so readily seen. An interesting feature of these cocoons is that they contain a long, unbroken thread of silk that is easily unreeled. At one time it could have been commercially valuable had labor been cheaper. The adult moths may be easily recognized by the windowlike spot on each wing. And while we are writing about these giant silkworm moths, we should briefly mention the larva, or caterpillar, of the *Io* moth, which is armed with venomous spines and thus should be handled carefully.

The Romans gave the name luna to the moon (luna being loosely derived from the Latin *lucere,* "to shine"), poetically styled the "fair empress of the night," and Luna was, of course, the moon goddess. So what could be more fitting than that the most beautiful of all our moths should be given the same name?

I saw my first living luna moth in the Maine woods. It was some years ago, and the evening was well advanced when, after reading for several hours, I felt the need to stretch my legs. I had no sooner emerged into the clearing in front of my cabin when I saw a fairly large, dark form fluttering about in the air and heading in the general direction of the lighted window. I was momentarily startled by the flying apparition, my mind still on the book I had been reading, and had not as yet collected my wits, in a manner of speaking, before I realized what it was. You can well imagine my elation on seeing a luna for the first time (I had seen any number of pinned specimens); though there were countless other moths and night-flying insects about the lighted window and on the screen, I had eyes for none but my unexpected and most welcome visitor.

Everyone is familiar with the story of the moth and the lighted candle. Unlike butterflies, which are attracted to sunlight but are repelled by artificial light, moths for the most part shun sunlight (though there are some species that fly about during the daylight hours) but are attracted to artificial light. It has been found that moths are not actually attracted by artificial light but are oriented by it and, in constantly adjusting their heads to the light, are drawn into it. In other words, when a moth flies in the vicinity of a light, the nervous controls of the insect automatically orient its body in flight so that the illumination is the same for both eyes, with the result that it flies toward the light. Often the results are fatal, as in the case of the moth and the candle.

If we cover one eye of a moth with an opaque coating of paint so that it can see with only one eye, the moth is no longer able to orient itself toward the light. Thus it is apparent that a moth does not fly toward a light because of curiosity but simply because it is under the control of its reflexes and must fly toward the light whether it wants to or not. Moths, however, are not attracted to lights of all intensities. They are repelled by those above and below certain intensities. This explains why moths do not fly toward the sun during the day or toward the full moon at night.

Most of us have observed the conspicuous and unsightly silken webs that suddenly seem to appear in early spring on such trees as the wild cherry. They are made by the tent caterpillar, and if you have no aversion to caterpillars in general, you will find it interesting to watch tent caterpillars feed and grow and gradually enlarge the size of their webs as they do so. Later they transform into small, dull yellowish or reddish brown moths.

Later on the silken webs of the fall webworm are equally as conspicuous on the September landscape. They are quite common on various trees but especially on apple and ash. Both the caterpillars and adult moths vary considerably in markings.

There are some one hundred species of dagger moths in North America. The name dagger refers to the daggerlike mark near the hind outer angle of the front wings, though this mark does not occur on all species. Sometimes in late summer or early fall we may see the caterpillar of the American dagger, densely clothed with yellow hairs, crawling along a city sidewalk looking for a place to pupate. And occasionally we might find hundreds of the red-humped apple worm on the blackberry bush though they are more commonly seen on the apple tree. They have a coral head and a hump of the same color on the first abdominal segment. Being gregarious, they often crowd so closely together that they completely cover the branch on which they are feeding. Mention of the apple worm calls to mind the beautiful white-marked tussock caterpillar, which has four white tussocks, three long pencils of white hair, and a coral red head. The tussock caterpillar may be found on various shade trees. The equally attractive hickory tiger moth caterpillar, has snowwhite and black-dotted tufts, and it occurs on the hickory, butternut, and other trees.

There are at least two hundred species of the Catocola moths in the United States, an interesting group of moths because they illustrate to a marked degree protective coloration. They generally have brilliantly colored hind wings of red, orange, and black. Their forewings, however, vary in color from white to gray and brown. In flight the moths are readily seen because of their brightly colored hind wings but when they alight or are at rest their forewings cover the hind wings, and the moths thus become inconspicuous. Indeed, they look so much like the bark of trees on which they usually rest that they become barely visible.

In many instances nice adjustments have to be made between plants and insects so that they may profit from each other. There are also many instances, however, where one profits at the expense of the other. Even then adjustments must be made, as in the case of the codling moth, which emerges from its cocoon when the apple trees blossom so that it may lay its eggs in time for the larvae to enter the young developing apples. The egg of the codling moth is a most curious object, flat and scalelike, about half the size of a pinhead, and so extremely thin and transparent that it is barely visible to the naked eye. In fact, it can be seen only by reflected light.

The codling moth is a major pest of the apple, and so is the spring cankerworm, though to a lesser degree. These are only two of the many species of moths that are destructive. Other prominent examples are the clothes moth, browntail moth, and gypsy moth, the last perhaps the most destructive of all, because it numbers almost five hundred different food plants in its dietary.

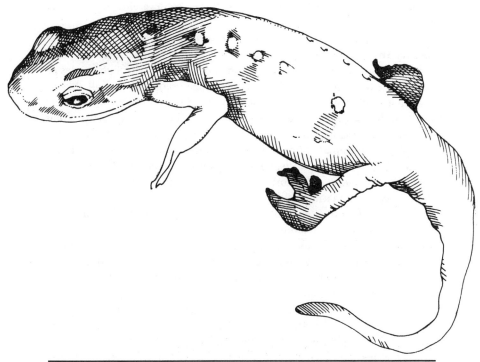

Eft/Spotted Newt
The double life

I used to delight in doing crossword puzzles, but lately I have rarely found the time to do one. Not that it matters too much, but I wonder if the three-letter word for a lizardlike animal is still as popular as it used to be. As perhaps you can guess, I am referring to the word *eft*.

Somehow the crossword puzzles always seemed to imply that the word *eft* referred to some mythical or rare animal. Yet the eft is neither mythical nor rare; on the contrary, it is fairly common though not often seen except after a rain. The reason is that the animal prefers damp or moist surroundings and during dry periods remains hidden among dead leaves, beneath a log or in some similar retreat.

After a rain or shower and even on foggy days it comes out

of its hiding place to forage for insects or whatever small animals it can find. Sometimes hundreds of them may be seen crawling along some road or woodland path or entering our gardens.

These efts may show great variation in color. Thus in one locality they may all be uniformly bright red, but in another the color may vary in different individuals from a dull reddish through shades of red orange to brilliant red. But whatever their color, they are all alike in having a single row of scarlet black-bordered dots on each side of their backs and a number of black specks here and there but especially along the sides, making them appear as if they had been peppered. The eft is a very pretty animal, but its greatest beauty is in its eyes, which are black, with elongated pupils, almost parallel with the length of the head and bordered close and below with bands of shining golden iris, which give them a fascinating brilliancy.

The eft is a small animal measuring not much more than two inches in length when fully grown. This includes the flattened tail, which it uses to right itself if it gets turned over on its back, as sometimes happens. The legs and feet do not seem adequate to support the body as they are short and set far apart, but it is surprising how fast the eft can move with them.

The eft is a timid animal and will often peer out at you from among the leaves with an expression that can best be described as alert shyness. Sometimes it will remain motionless for so long that it might appear as if carved out of stone; then suddenly it will spring into life and dart away with lightning speed, its body falling into graceful curves as it moves along.

The eft is not a fully developed or mature animal but rather the young stage of a salamander called the spotted newt, which has an entirely different color scheme and moreover lives entirely in water. So from the viewpoint of color and habitat they would appear to be two distinct animals, although they are actually but two different color phases of the same animal.

The spotted newt has a very interesting life history, which consists of three stages: the larval stage, which is spent in the water, the young red, or *eft*, stage, which is spent on land, and the adult, or *spotted newt*, stage which is also spent in the water.

Let us briefly trace this unique life history. The red efts live on land until they become mature and are ready to return to the water whence they came. The size and age at which they mature depend on various factors. In some localities it may take as long as three years for them to mature, in others but one year. The average length of time appears, however, to be two years.

At any rate, as soon as they become mature, they feel the urge to take up a water-dwelling existence. They assemble from all directions and begin moving to a pond or stream. Although they may be far from any body of water they seem to know instinctively where to go. Over the ground, through tall grass, over and around obstacles of all kinds, the little efts crawl and crawl with a persistency that seems to be beyond the powers of such small animals. At last they reach the water that is to be their home for the rest of their lives.

Then, if they have not already done so, they change their color to that of the adults, becoming olive brown above and buff below but still retaining the pepperlike spots and the red spots along the back. Minor structural changes also take place, but these do not greatly change the form of the little efts.

The little red efts are now no longer the little red efts but adult newts. They are still the same animal but with a new interest in life—to mate. Mating takes place chiefly during March and April but may occur throughout the entire year. After a rather elaborate courtship, the eggs are laid. Eggs are about the size of a pea, are brown at one end and creamy white at the other, and are surrounded with a jelly cover. They are laid singly, usually in the axils of leaves and stems of such pond plants as elodea and chara, and in a little less than a month hatch into larvae, which are quite different from the red efts. They are green, with gray stripes along their sides and three tiny bunches of red gills on each side, just back of the head, and they have a long, thin, fishlike tail.

The larvae are expert swimmers and breathe in the manner of a fish. They remain in the water throughout the succeeding months, feeding on small worms, insects, and small mollusks and by the middle of August have developed lungs. As a matter of fact, they have changed so completely that they are no longer fitted to live in water and shortly leave it to take up a terrestrial existence. They have also changed their color to a brick red and in short have become the little red efts.

Muskrat
The house builder

As we drive through the country in late summer or early fall, taking advantage of the few remaining pleasant days before the stormy ones of winter drive us to our fireside, we are likely to notice, if we are observant, conical piles of mud and vegetable matter rising above the water in swampy and marshy areas. They look so much like natural hummocks that we may give them but a passing thought. They are, however, winter lodges of the muskrats, and if we have a moment we may well stop and examine them, if only at a distance.

The muskrat houses are usually dome shaped, although they vary in different parts of the country. As a rule they are two or three feet high but may be as high as four feet, with a diameter of ten feet. The animals may build their houses among willow sprouts or in masses of sweet flags, but they usually select a site where the water is about two feet deep, either in the middle of a stream or a few feet offshore in a pond. At this spot they bring together sedges, pondweeds, cattails, and other coarse vegetation, which they mix with mud. This material becomes more or less immovable as it continues to pile up. When they have a pile sufficiently large, the muskrats then make a tunnel or plunge hold from the bottom upward and hollow out a chamber below the surface of the dome. Meanwhile, as the roof sinks, more mud and stalks are placed on the top of the chamber. The entire house is finally wadded and plastered with mud and water-soaked small vegetation until the entire structure is firm and able to withstand the buffeting of winter storms.

The chamber, which is carpeted with a soft bed of leaves and moss, may be a foot or more in diameter. It is sufficiently high to enable the occupants to move about freely. Since it serves as both feeding and sleeping quarters, it may contain several alcoves slightly partitioned from one another, or there may be two chambers, each with its own plunge hold. Such chambers are probably occupied by different families. As a rule, the largest houses rarely provide quarters for more than five or six muskrats, but there is a case on record where an enormous lodge harbored fourteen animals.

All muskrats do not build these winter lodges. If the banks of the pond or stream that they inhabit are suitable, they instead tunnel into the banks beneath the water, slanting upward, and construct a chamber well above high-water level, which they line and use as a winter retreat. In either case the muskrats are active all winter, making excursions beneath the ice and feeding on submerged roots and stalks of lilies, cattails, and other water plants. They often travel great distances beneath the ice, and wherever they find openings they build eating huts over them.

Should a severe winter follow a dry fall and the ponds and streams freeze to the bottom, the animals may be frozen into their houses or shut out on land, to be starved or killed by their enemies. Or should the water rise, they may be forced to leave their houses and search for new locations, a hazardous undertaking, as they are thus exposed to attack.

But despite such dangers, muskrats dwell in comparative safety during the winter, for the ice protects them from all enemies except the mink. Whatever the weather may be above the ice, the temperature in their retreats hardly varies a degree. Snow or sleet storms may howl through the swamps and marshes, and foxes and owls may range the frozen sloughs, but as long as the ice holds, the muskrats come and go as they please. They have no lack of air, for there is usually enough close up under the edge of the bank. There may also be stretches of unfrozen water where they may swim with their heads out of water as in summer, breathing as they go. Here, of course, danger may lurk in the form of a mink, which has come to fish but is ever ready to seize any unwary muskrat that happens its way.

Although amphibious, the muskrats are more at home in the water than on land and are found wherever water and food plants provide suitable conditions for living. Unlike the wild and retiring beavers, they have adapted their habits to the presence of man and carry on their daily activities with complete indifference as to how he may view them. Indeed, they may often be found within a short distance of anyone's house.

Muskrats are essentially nocturnal in their habits and do most of their hunting for food at night. Nevertheless, I have seen them during the day, especially in summer, when they delight in swimming or floating in the shadow of old willows, where the water is deep and cool. I have marvelled at how easily they swim, with their noses or heads and the tips of their tails above the water. They always believe in safety first and often avoid such enemies as the fox by building little islands or rafts of sticks, cattails, and other plant stalks on which they sit while feeding. From such rafts they plunge headlong into the water upon the approach of an enemy. In winter the rafts are not always completely covered by ice but may be roofed over with snow. They then serve as breathing holes when the animals are swimming under the ice in search of food.

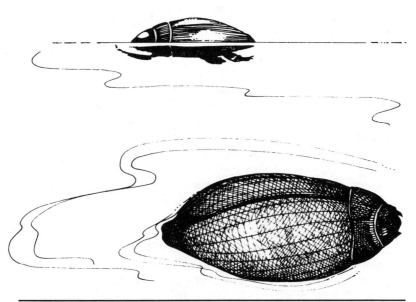

Whirligig Beetles
The whirligigs

I can't recall how old I was when I first began to roam the countryside exploring the fields and meadows and woodlands that were all in the immediate vicinity of where I lived, as any curious and inquisitive boy would do. And it doesn't really matter. About a stone's throw from our house a brook meandered its way to the river into which it flowed. There I would often go to watch the dragonflies course up and down along the stream's edge performing their aerial acrobatics, the weaker flying damsel flies that often flew in tandem, and the thin-legged crane flies—all of them casting moving shadows on the water. There I would also watch the backswimmers and water boatmen and the diving beetles swimming and diving in the water, the water scavenger beetles and

water scorpions crawling along the bottom, and the water skaters gliding over the surface as well as the ever present whirligigs that imitated
whirling dervishes in their seemingly mad gyrations.

Anyone who has ever wandered about our ponds and
streams has seen the whirligigs at some time or other and doubtless has
stopped to watch them as they swam about on the surface of the water.
They are the small steel blue or black beetles that may be found in
almost any brook or quiet pond, and they may be seen at almost any
time of the year except when the brooks and ponds are frozen over. But
it is in early spring, when rising temperatures lure them from the mud
in which they have spent the winter, that they appear in the largest
numbers, gyrating on the surface and breaking the water into ripples,
or basking like turtles on logs and stones. If alarmed or disturbed, they
dash about in interlacing circles, and so quickly do they move that the
eye cannot follow any single one in its mad turnings and twistings.
Occasionally they fly, if they can climb out of the water to take off.
When captured, they squeak by rubbing the tip of their abdomen
against the wings, and they emit a disagreeable milky fluid.

No matter how many there are or how fast they swim, they
never collide as they dart about and around each other, nor do they
bump into objects like floating sticks or protruding rocks or logs. Even
if a number of them are transferred to the surface of an aquarium, there
are still no collisions. Darken a room and illuminate the aquarium with
a red light, such as a photographer's darkroom lamp, to which the
beetles do not respond, and they will still not collide. However, remove
all dust from the surface of the water by skimming it several times with
the sharp edge of a glass plate, or coat the inside walls of the aquarium
with paraffin so that the water meniscus disappears, and they will not
only swim into each other but will also bump the glass walls.

The answer to this apparent mystery is a simple one. As the
beetles swim on the surface of the water, they set in motion floating
particles of various kinds that in turn give rise to vibrations. The beetles
are able to detect these vibrations, as well as those reflected from
objects in the water and on the shore, and thus avoid collisions in
somewhat the same manner that bats avoid colliding with objects by
echolocation. The organ that appears sensitive to these vibrations is
called Johnston's organ, a minute and complex structure composed
mainly of tactile hairs and located on the second antennal segment.
Remove this organ and collisions will occur.

Examine a whirligig carefully, and you will readily see why
it is such a capable swimmer. Note how the body is flattened out, oval,

and smooth, a design that helps the insect to overcome the resistance of the water. In some species (there are about thirty, which differ from one another mainly in length and color pattern) the ventral, or lower, surface is shaped like a canoe, allowing the insect to move through the water with even greater facility. Observe, too, how the hind legs, fringed with hairs and shaped like paddles, are used as oars to drive the insect through the water in a rapid sculling movement. Also look closely at the eyes with a hand lens; you will find that they are divided by the sharp margin of the head so that the insect can look up from the water with one half of the eye and down into it with the other half. Whirligigs frequently dive. When they do they carry down with them a bubble of air under the tips of the wing covers. It glistens like a ball of silver and is easily seen.

Ballooning Spiders
The balloonists

The thought that spiders can go ballooning through the air might at first seem preposterous, but on reflection, perhaps not. Spiders spin silk, so what is to prevent them from spinning silken parachutes to carry them through the air? And that is exactly what happens with the ballooning spiders.

We can see ballooning spiders throughout the year, but they are most numerous in the spring and the fall, when large numbers hatch from the egg and emerge from the egg sac to fly. I have seen them more often in the fall, on a soft October day when the sun shines brightly and a gentle breeze flows over the landscape. At such a time countless miniature parachutes may be seen floating through the air.

To the uninitiated they would appear to be carrying some kind of seed—perhaps milkweed, dandelion, or thistle. But if one of these parachutes is examined closely, it will be seen to be carrying a small spider, or spiderling.

Humans take considerable pride, and well may they do so, in what they have accomplished in solving the problems of aerial navigation, but spiders have been sailing through the air for a long, long time, perhaps ever since they first appeared on the earth. Their method of doing so may not be on the high technical level of our modern airliners but it gets them places, and over the years—or should we say eons—has proved quite satisfactory; I doubt if a spider would want to change even if given the chance to do so.

When a spider feels the urge to go sailing through the air, it climbs to the summit of some elevated object—a plant, a grass spike, a fence post or rail—and faces the direction of the wind. Then it extends its eight legs, four on each side, and lifts its abdomen to an angle of about forty-five degrees so that its body is raised above its perch.

At the tip of the abdomen and beneath it are the spinnerets, fingerlike appendages that are covered with minute spinning spools through which jets of silk are now forced from a multitude of glands within the body. The liquid silk hardens on contact with the air in the form of threads that are seized and drawn out by the air currents to a length of sometimes as much as twenty feet.

These threads are held apart or are combined at the spider's will by the closing or outspreading of the spinnerets. Meanwhile, as the threads are carried out by the air currents, the spider's legs are inclined toward the breeze, and the joints stiffen, the entire attitude of the spider showing the muscular strain to which it is subjected by resisting the uplifting force.

The spider continues the spinning process until it instinctively knows that this uplifting force is sufficient to support it in the air. Then it disengages its feet from its perch and takes off, to float in the air in whichever direction the air currents will carry it.

The spider is not, however, completely at the mercy of the air currents, as one might suppose, but is able to exercise a certain amount of control over its "balloon" by climbing about the silken threads and pulling in and winding up the silken filaments or spinning more of them.

Small spiders, or spiderlings, may often be made to take off by blowing steadily against them, and sometimes very tiny spiders, weighing very little, are suddenly lifted into the air by the air currents when they least expect it. Even the larger spiders are frequently caught by the wind when dropping on their draglines and are blown no inconsiderable distance.

The ballooning generally goes on at heights up to two hundred feet, but powerful air currents often carry the small aeronauts as high as ten thousand feet. The object of the flights that the spiders take is presumed to be a dispersal of the species, and there is no doubt that the system is effective. That the ballooning spiders are often carried considerable distances is shown by the fact that they have been picked up by ships at sea several hundred miles from land.

Sometimes spiders attempt to balloon when the wind is too strong, and then the threads that they have spun are not lifted up but instead are blown against some object; then large fields are often covered with a gauze of silk. At other times sheets of silk are formed by the massing together of myriad strands. The sheets are finally torn away by the wind and later deposited elsewhere, producing the showers of gossamer celebrated in prose and poetry.

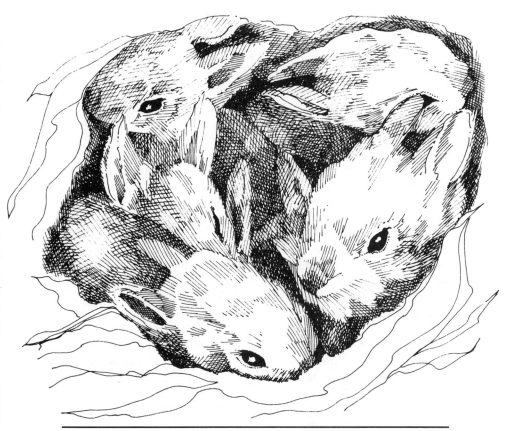

Cottontail Rabbit
The inhabitant of the hedgerow

Few animals of our fields and forests have as many enemies as the cottontail rabbit. Hawks, owls, skunks, foxes, red squirrels, weasels, mink, snakes—indeed all predatory animals that can catch the cottontail consider it legitimate prey; and then there are your hunters, who with the odds overwhelmingly in their favor hunt it in the name of what they like to call sport. Which calls to mind the following:

> *The bunnies are a feeble folk whose*
> *weakness is their strength.*
> *To shun a gun a bun will run to*
> *almost any length.*

Every year millions of these little animals lose their lives, and if Nature in her omniscience had not made them prolific breeders, they would long since have gone the way of the dodo, the passenger pigeon, the heath hen, and all the other species that have vanished from the face of the earth. Yet in spite of its many enemies, natural or otherwise, the cottontail lives and flourishes in our midst, which is as it should be.

Anyone not overly familiar with this little inhabitant of the briar patch and hedgerow might think that it is wholly defenseless against such relentless enemies as the hawk, weasel, and fox and the other larger carnivorous mammals, to say nothing of humans, with their modern high-powered rifles. That is not so, of course. I doubt very much if any animal that Nature created is without some means of defense, although in the case of the cottontail its means of protection are probably not too successful.

More than one cottontail has owed its life to its colors, which so blend with the animal's surroundings that it easily escapes detection, even by such sharp-eyed enemies as the hawks. Also its habit of "freezing," or remaining perfectly motionless except for a trembling of its whiskers and the almost imperceptible movement of breathing, often serves it in good stead. I have seen a cottontail "freeze," and no amount of staring at it would seem to disconcert it or put it out of countenance, although I will admit that on being approached too closely, it quickly raced away.

The cottontail is by nature a timid animal and at the slightest indication of danger will usually seek safety beneath some cover. It can travel with considerable speed over the ground, its long hind legs propelling it forward in a series of jumps that sometimes cover a distance of eight feet or more. But it has none of the specializations for speed of the jack rabbit and depends for its safety more on the protection afforded by the undergrowth or some other retreat than on flight. Especially during the colder months, it often uses the deserted burrow of a woodchuck or skunk as a refuge in which to spend the daylight hours or as a place of safety in time of danger. Sometimes, though, such a retreat fails as a sanctuary, particularly if it is pursued by a mink or weasel, for these animals can go through any opening that will admit the rabbit.

It is questionable whether many of these animals succeed in following a cottontail to its burrow. As a rule the cottontail when pursued makes use of the runways leading to the burrow, and these runways crisscross and twist and turn so much that the rabbit can usually elude any pursuer, at least long enough to seek a place of safety.

Yet the goshawk has the habit in winter of following these paths on foot in a most unhawklike manner. When the paths are made in tangled undergrowth, the hawk is prevented from soaring down from above, so it resorts to tracking the rabbit until it can scare the rabbit out into the open—where its mate will be waiting. (Goshawks generally hunt in pairs during the winter.)

How little some people know about rabbits! I have often seen some well-intentioned but misguided person pick up a rabbit by its ears, as if Nature meant that the long ears were to serve as handles. Nature designed the rabbit's ears for the same purpose as ours and other animals' and in the case of the rabbit made them especially long, so that it might hear the approach of an enemy in time to seek safety. The long legs and long ears are the rabbit's means of defense. True, they are a negative sort of defense, depending on retreat rather than attack. And yet a rabbit will attack if cornered, jumping over its enemy and kicking it fiercely on the back with its strong hind feet. Ernest Thompson Seton, well-known naturalist and writer, tells of a rabbit that got the best of a black snake in this manner.

I have often come upon a cottontail during the day, although it is really a night prowler, preferring to remain during the daylight hours in a "form" under the protecting cover of a blackberry thicket, in a grass tussock, or at the base of a tree. I have lived most of my life in New England, where the cottontails are most at home in open woods, brush-grown pastures with fringing woods, and briar-grown berry patches and thickets. In such haunts we may see them as the shades of dusk begin to fall, emerging from their hiding places and scampering merrily over the ground in search of tender green vegetation on which they love to feed.

On many a moonlit night I have suddenly come upon one of these little fellows sitting on its hind legs and with ears erect upon my approach. Then as I made some sound that startled it, it would turn and dash from view, its little white pompom of a tail waving defiance.

The cottontail feeds on buds, leaves, berries, green twigs, and bark, being especially fond of sumac bark, to say nothing of garden vegetables when convenient, and thus perhaps becoming a nuisance through levelling early summer crops.

Unlike the squirrel, the cottontail cannot use its front legs as hands when feeding. The front legs of the cottontail have a peculiarity in that the bones are so arranged that the legs cannot be turned inward and thus used as hands. And though the cottontail may raise the fore part of its body clear of the ground when reaching upward to feed, the fore legs hang useless at such a time.

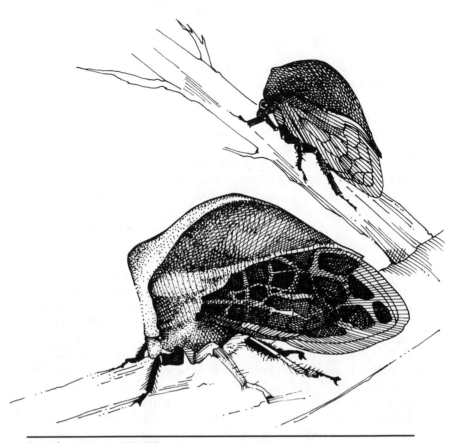

Tree Hoppers
A matter of change

Nature works in many strange and diverse ways, and there is no better example of this than the group of insects known as the tree hoppers. In this group of insects she has taken a simple structure and changed it into many weird forms.

Tree hoppers are so named because most of the species live on trees and hop vigorously when disturbed. Some species, however, live on low shrubs, grasses, and other herbaceous plants. They all suck plant juices, and the eggs are usually laid in the tissues of the plants. Rarely do they occur in sufficient numbers to be of any economic import though occasionally the females may injure young trees by laying their eggs in the bark of the smaller branches and in the buds.

Many tree hoppers excrete a liquid called honeydew, which is eagerly sought by the ants and as a result are attended by them.

The tree hoppers have been called the insect brownies. If you want to know why, look at a number of species full in the face, and the reason will be quite apparent. Should you do so, you will see how a simple structure has been modified in a variety of ways. Note how the prothorax—the part of the thorax that bears the front legs—has been prolonged backward above the abdomen and how, in some species, it is extended sidewise or upward as well. The American entomologist John Henry Comstock once remarked that "nature must have been in a joking mood when tree hoppers were developed." Nature, however, plans nothing idly and had another intent when she started to play with the prothorax, for the majority of modifications are contrived to promote protective resemblance: Thus many tree hoppers look like plant structures, such as buds or thorns, and are as a result left alone by birds and other insectivorous animals.

There is, for instance, an interesting species that lives upon bittersweet, the hoppers looking so much like thorns that it is difficult to distinguish them. Only when they suddenly galvanize into action can we be sure of their identity. They appear to be a diminutive flock of fowl and perch, no matter how the vine twists and turns, with their heads always toward the top. They rest in such a manner so that the sap they suck can flow more easily down their tiny throats. In the fall cottony tufts may be found on the vine. These are protective coverings constructed to keep the eggs they deposited in the bark safe from the snows and icy blasts of winter.

This tree hopper is known popularly as the two-marked tree-hopper in reference to the two yellow spots on the dorsal line of the pronotum. When seen through a magnifying glass, it bears a fanciful resemblance to the partridge. Many, many years ago it was the subject of a charming article written by William Hamilton Gibson, "A Queer Little Family on the Bitter-Sweet," published in *Harper's Monthly* for August, 1892.

Another common tree hopper is a little hump-backed species that is often found on the branches of Virginia creeper. And another is found upon the leaves of sunflowers. Probably of the greatest economic consequence is the one popularly called the buffalo tree-hopper because of its supposed similarity to the buffalo (bison). This insect is often injurious to young orchard trees, especially apples, because of the punctures the female makes in the bark with her sawlike ovipositor, or egg-laying device, in order to lay her eggs.

A related species, the two-horned tree-hopper, resembles the buffalo tree-hopper in both size and form. It is a pale dirty yellow, spotted with brown, and is densely clothed with hairs. It is common on black elder.

Bluebird, Robin, and Other Songbirds
The spring heralds

When I lived in New England, the end of February invariably found me afield as often as time permitted, attentive to the first signs of a returning spring. It may have been the lovely hepatica hidden away in a woodland nook, or the call of the spring peeper issuing from the unfrozen water around the rim of a still ice-covered pond, or the glimpse of blue among the naked branches of a roadside maple or the apple tree in the orchard. And then I knew that spring was on its way. The bluebird, with his soft warble and gentle manners, was once again with us.

We welcome this lovable bird, which is not as common as it used to be, with genuine warmth, for with the exception of the robin, no other bird shows such a decided fondness for human society. Place a birdhouse on a nearby tree or on a tall post, and he will quickly become its tenant and throughout the following weeks will reward you with many happy moments for having provided him with a readymade home.

He is one of our truly useful birds, too. No one has been able to accuse him of stealing fruit or eating our crops. His diet consists mostly of insects, and such vegetable food as he does eat is of little use to us. One whose orchard is overrun with harmful insects would do well to cultivate his friendship.

In New England the bluebird was the first of the migratory song birds to return from the South, but a day or two later I was sure to see a robin on the lawn or hear his sharp clucking call from a nearby tree. For some reason the first robin of spring always seems to be alone. Yet a day or two later he may be seen in company with several others as if they had been close at hand but timid about putting in an appearance. That seems unlikely, however, for the robin shows a most charming confidence in the friendliness of man and instinctively seems to know we mean him no harm. He walks unconcernedly about our lawns in search of worms and often builds his nest and rears his family on the woodwork or in the vines of a porch or in a tree within a few feet of a window or door.

It might be days before the robin began to sing. Then suddenly some early morning I would hear his simple song of faith and hope. But even before the robin burst into song, the song sparrow had already begun to sound his gay carol from every quarter. This little feathered songster seems to care little about the weather. Once he starts to sing, he will perform on the brightest morning or the bleakest day, even though chill winds may blow and snow and ice still decorate the landscape. He will pour out his liveliest carol in a spirit of optimism and in defiance of the raging elements as if to speed departing winter on its way.

March in New England is a capricious month; we never knew what the weather would be from day to day. There may be several days of sunny warm weather, and then a snowstorm will blanket the landscape. For the most part it is a chilly month with blustering winds that sweep over the fields and meadows and through the still leafless woods. It would seem that our feathered wanderers would be deterred from returning too soon from warmer parts. But March with all its vagaries of weather apparently holds no terrors for them. Shortly after we saw the bluebird and robin, which usually put in their appearance during the first week, we would hear the familiar note of the phoebe about the barn, in the orchard, and along the rushing stream and invariably see the tail-wagging bird itself. And in the marsh we would see the male redwings, their scarlet epaulets conspicuous against the background of lustrous black, perched on the swaying rushes and giving voice to their raucous "kong-quer-ree."

Then suddenly one day we would see the grackles whirling into a leafless tree, their iridescent plumage twinkling greens and purples in the dancing sunbeams, advertising their return by discordant chatterings. And before the month was out we would see a marsh hawk sail out of the blue sky in his buoyant and unhurried manner and a cowbird, notorious for its belief in free love, fly out from among the shadows and strut over the ground like some silent phantom. Perhaps we would also hear the few notes of the fox sparrow, the handsomest and largest of our sparrows, whose song is like the soft tinkling of tiny silver bells, or we might hear his noisy scratching in a thicket as he searched for still dormant insects.

As the month came to a close, we would also likely see the vesper sparrow running along a country road, flirting his white-tipped tail where the whitlow grass blooms as a meadowlark called from a still brown field.

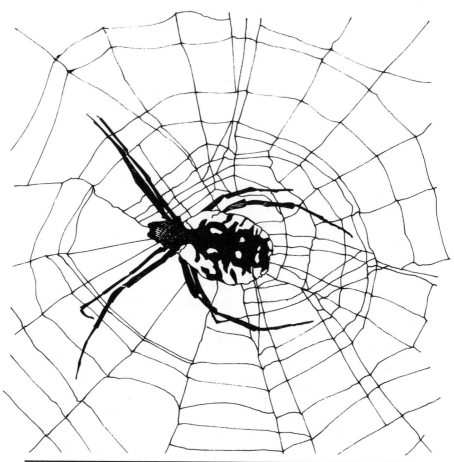

Web-Spinning Spiders
The nonpareil engineer

On a summer's morning a heavy condensation of dew may bring out in
bold relief the countless webs of the grass spider. Few of us realize what
an immense number of webs are spun by this species upon the grass.
When dew condenses upon them and makes them visible, the fields and
our lawns appear to be covered with an almost continuous carpet of
silk, calling to mind the following:

> And dew-bright webs festoon the grass
> In roadside fields at morning.

The web of the grass spider is shaped somewhat in the form of a broad funnel with a tube extending downward at one side. This tube is used by the spider as a hideout or retreat in which to lie in wait for its prey and or hide from its enemies. In spinning this tubular retreat, the spider, with considerable foresight, does not close the tube up and thus make a cul-de-sac of it from which no escape would be possible. Instead, it leaves the tube open so that it may, if necessary, leave its web through a back door.

Many lines of silk, which cross each other irregularly, compose the web of the grass spider. Collectively they form a firm sheet, which is held in place by many guy lines that are attached to grass stems. There is usually, above the sheet, an irregular open network of silken threads to catch flying insects or so impede their flight that they will tumble or fall upon the sheet. There they can be seized by the waiting spider. Touch the web slightly, and you will see the spider spring out from its hiding place intent upon seizing some unfortunate victim, but jar the web roughly, and the spider will take fright instead and speed out through the back door.

Originally, eons ago, spiders used silk only to wrap up their masses of eggs. Then they took to lining their retreats with it, and after a while they began to use it in building platforms outside the retreats. From here it was but a step to use the silk in constructing snares, which must have been very primitive. As time went on, the snares gradually developed into the ones which now so excite our wonder and admiration.

The snares of spiders differ greatly. They may be merely a maze of threads extending in all directions, such as those built by the domestic or house spider and which we commonly refer to as cobwebs; or they may be a more or less closely woven sheet extended in a single plane and consisting of threads extending in all directions with no apparent regularity or arrangement, like those built by the hammock spider. Finer workmanship is seen in the funnel-shaped webs of the grass spider and in webs of the orb type, perhaps the most intricate and exquisite structures made by any of the lower animals.

Orb webs vary greatly in structure, according to the species, but fundamentally they are all alike in that the central portion—the part lying within the supporting framework—consists of a series of radiating lines of dry silk and inelastic silk, which are banded by circumferential lines of viscid and elastic silk. One of the largest of the orb webs—sometimes measuring two feet in diameter—is that made by the garden spider, a species an inch or more long and marked with spots and bands of bright orange. This is the beautiful spider that we may find in late summer spinning its web on herbaceous growth in fields, along roadsides, and even in our gardens.

To watch a spider, especially an orb weaver such as the garden spider, spin its web is a never-to-be-forgotten experience. I have before me some notes I jotted down some years ago when I was curious to learn just how a spider goes about its business of spinning a web. The spider I selected for observation was one that had already built a web between two neighboring shrubs. I ruthlessly demolished this web so that she would have to build a new one.

When beginning her operations, the spider climbed out to the tip of a branch. There, lifting up her abdomen so that the thread would not become entangled among the leaves and branches, she spun out a thread of silk, which was carried by the air currents toward the other shrub in which it caught. The spider, thereupon, pulled in the slack and fastened the silken thread securely to the branch on which she was standing, using a number of minute looped threads collectively called an attachment disc.

The spider now had a bridge over which she could cross to the other shrub. Her next step was to strengthen this bridge, which she accomplished by passing back and forth over it several times, each time adding a strand of silk to it. When she had reinforced the bridge to her satisfaction, she let herself down by means of a thread of silk, called the dragline, to a branch below one end of the bridge and there fastened the strand in place, thus completing two sides of the outer framework of her web.

Here she paused for a moment. When she resumed her labors, she climbed back up this perpendicular strand, crossed the bridge, and at the other end again lowered herself until she reached a point opposite to what was to be the lower right-hand corner of her framework. She fastened this second dragline in place, and then spinning a thread as she went she climbed up this dragline to the bridge, crossed over, and descended the first dragline until she reached the point where it was attached to the branch.

Here she pulled in the slack and fastened it. The four sides of the framework were now completed. The strands, called foundation lines, I might add, did not form a perfect rectangle but left an open space more or less irregular in outline in which she was to construct her web.

With her foundation lines now all in place, the spider next proceeded to build the orb. She made her way to the original bridge, crossed half way over, and fastened a strand of silk in place. Then by means of this dragline she lowered herself to the second bridge to which she fastened it. She now climbed back up the dragline, which passed through a point that was to be the center of her orb, and when she reached that central point (how she knew when she got to it we can only guess), she fastened another thread of silk. Then spinning, she continued to climb until she reached the bridge. She crossed part way to one end and there fastened the line she was spinning, thus putting in place the first radiating line, or radius, of the orb.

Incidentally, it was interesting to observe that while spinning the thread as she made her way along the silken strands, she held it up behind her so that it would not become entangled in the strands using both hind feet for the purpose.

With her first radius in place, she returned to the center of the orb, attached another strand of silk, and repeated the operation until she had fastened a second radius. She repeated the operation a third time and a fourth and stopped only when she had constructed all her radiating lines. She did not, however, put all these radii in place in regular succession. Instead she built first on one side and then on another, apparently to avoid putting too much strain on one side of the frame.

When she finally had all the radii in place, she proceeded to strengthen the center of the web, the point at which the radii converged, by spinning a mesh or network of lines called the hub. This hub was to serve as her future headquarters. Then she began to spin a spiral band from the hub onward, spinning it over the entire area to be covered by the orb and at right angles to the radii. The purpose of this spiral line was merely to hold the radii in place for future operations.

So far all the lines or threads that the spider had spun, except those she used to fasten the threads in place, were dry and inelastic. But now, going to the outer margin of the orb, she began to spin a sticky, threadlike substance—I could see it streaming from her spinnerets, glistening like dew—which she fastened to one of the radii by means of an attachment disk. She then went on to another radius, pulling out the thread from her spinnerets. Before she fastened the thread to the radius, she took hold of it with a spine of one hind leg and, straightening out the leg, pulled out from the spinnerets more of the thread.

The spinnerets were then applied to the radius and the thread fastened in place. The spider removed her hind leg, whereupon the thread contracted to the length of the space between the two radii.

The reason for pulling out the sticky or viscid line between the two radii was to leave it relaxed when put in place so that it could easily be stretched by an entangled insect and thus ensure its being caught in other turns of the sticky spiral.

In spinning the viscid spiral, the spider did not pass around the entire web but first made a few loops on the lower part of it. Then she proceeded to go around it, gradually making her way to the center. When she came to the temporary spiral reinforcement, she cut it away, much as a tailor might remove basting threads. As I watched her work, I could not help but be amazed at the uncanny skill with which this nonpareil engineer measured angles and calculated stresses and strains without ever having been shown how.

At last, after several hours of toil, she completed the exquisite structure. I was left with the feeling that I had just witnessed some strange and inexplicable phenomenon, as in truth I had.

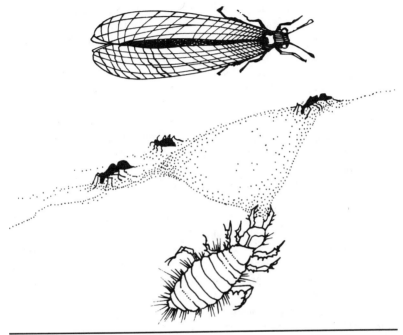

Ant Lion
The pit digger

There is considerable diversity in the way predatory animals get their prey: Some of them pursue it, others lie in wait and then pounce upon it, and still others contrive traps and snares—as the ant lion does.

I don't know why the ant lion is called an ant lion. Its habits are totally unlike those of the four-footed animal from which it gets part of its name, except that it is predatory. The *ant* part of its name is consistent with its habits, however, as it feeds chiefly on these insects.

The ant lion, which occurs in sandy areas such as under rocky ledges, below shed roofs, and about houses, is a most curious-looking creature, with a humped back, a long tapering abdomen, and a sneaky-appearing head from which project fierce jaws. The front pair of legs are small and spiny and are quite unlike the strong hind ones, which are twisted, with sharp-spiked claws that serve to push the animal vigorously forward should the need for such movement occur.

The trap of the "lion" is a pit, which the insect always digs in sand or in loose soil and in a place that is secluded from the wind and rain. Having selected such a site, it begins digging its trap by first excavating a circular groove in the sand. Within this groove it excavates another and then another and so on until it has fashioned a conical pit, the size varying with the size of the animal. Sometimes the pit is less than an inch across, while at other times it may be as much as two inches in diameter.

The "lion" digs in a rather quaint manner, scraping the sand on its head by means of its front legs and then jerking its head suddenly upward, thus throwing the sand quite a distance. Upon completing its pit, it digs in at the bottom and there lies in wait for a victim, all that is visible of the "lion" being a pair of long curved jaws.

The secret of the ant lion's trap is that the sand on the sides lies at such an angle that the least disturbance causes it to slide toward the bottom. Thus the moment an ant steps over the edge of the pit it begins to slide toward the bottom, where the ant lion is lying in wait to receive it. Should the ant by vigorous struggling manage to stop its descent and seem likely to escape, the "lion" goes into action and throws up little showers of sand. The sand falls on the struggling ant, knocks it down, and precipitates its descent into eternity.

Should the ant, however, be strong and powerful a tug-of-war is likely to ensue between the two antagonists. In such a struggle, the "lion" is usually the victor, for its crooked hind legs serve to anchor it in its pit until the ant becomes weakened through struggling, when it becomes an easy prey. After the ant-lion has feasted, the remains of its dinner are thrown out in the same manner as the sand.

The ant lion can undergo long fasts, and here we have another interesting provision of Nature. As the ant lion must lie in wait for a meal to come along, days and even weeks may pass before it eats. Accordingly, the length of an ant lion's life varies with the food supply. Thus it may take anywhere from one year to three years for the "lion" to become full grown. When this time comes, the ant-lion fashions a loose and globular cocoon of silk and sand, pupates, and emerges as a delicate, gauzy-winged insect wholly unlike the ferocious animal that lay hidden in its cunningly devised trap.

Birds' Nests
The cradles of the music makers

The year has four seasons. In some parts of the country, as in the Northeast and the Midwest, they are distinctive and have their own character. In autumn, for instance, which is the time of leaf fall, the trees become naked and, silhouetted against the sky, reveal their individual architecture. Myriads of birds' nests, practically invisible a few short weeks before except perhaps to a discerning eye, now stand out in bold relief. Then I will find the nest of the catbirds that I searched for in vain in a dense roadside thicket not too long ago. The nest of the wood thrush, too, a bird whose bell-like notes issued from the nearby woods and fell upon the silent country air on warm June nights like some wandering strain from another world, will become exposed. Even the exquisite basket of the oriole, swinging in the autumn breeze from the drooping branch of a towering elm, will be more in evidence.

I must confess that at one time a nest to me was merely a mass of heterogeneous materials, ingeniously put together to be sure, but of no value except to the bird that made it. One nest seemed very much like another. But I have since discovered that nests are not the prosaic things they appear to be and that they are not all alike; they vary in shape and size, in the kind of materials used, and in location as much as the birds themselves vary in size, coloration, and habits. I also discovered that the study of birds' nests can be a rewarding and fascinating pastime and that it is not difficult to learn to identify them. Their makers follow more or less definite patterns; with a little practice one can become adept at identification.

Birds build nests primarily to serve as cradles for their young and as a means of holding their young together until they are able to take care of themselves. Moreover, since it is essential that the young be reared to maturity, birds select sites for their nests with the greatest care. They do not build simply in the most convenient place, or wherever their fancy may lead them, but they select sites that are accessible to feeding grounds, offer protection against the elements, and are well concealed from their natural enemies. Yet in spite of the extreme care that the birds exercise in selecting their nesting sites, so many dangers continually beset them that it is doubtful if one in ten of the nests that are started succeed in housing the young to maturity.

The males actually do no building but only make a pretence of doing so. To be sure, they select the general nesting area, but it is the females that choose the site where the nest is to be built and who do most, if not all, of the building. Once, I recall, I observed a male house wren carrying a stick for nest building. I don't know how many sticks the bird had collected or would continue to collect, or where he had built his nest. In any event, he could have saved himself the trouble, for his mate could use neither the sticks nor the nest. He was, however, merely performing an age-old ritual, for the practice of building "dummy nests" is a part of the house wren's courtship ceremony. The male arrives earlier than the female and, while waiting for her, spends his time filling every nesting box and cranny in the nesting area with sticks and even building well-shaped nests. But his mate will have no part of any nest that he may have built. She builds her own with materials that they both gather and in a place that she herself selects.

Birds build their nests in almost every conceivable location. The song sparrow may make its nest beneath a tuft of grass, the great blue heron in the tallest tree, the chimney swift in a chimney, the yellow warbler in a low bush, the black-capped chickadee in a decaying stump, the house sparrow in an electric light hood or water spout, the osprey on a crossbar of a telephone pole, the crested flycatcher in a hole in a tree, the kingfisher in a burrow in a sandbank, and the house wren in the most unlikely places—an old tin can, the fold of a blanket hanging on a clothes line, or the burrow in a bank made by a bank swallow for its nesting.

Not only do nesting sites vary, but the nests themselves vary from very crude structures to quite elaborate affairs. Thus the mourning dove builds merely a loose platform of twigs. The yellow-billed cuckoo does only slightly better. Its nest is little more than a shallow, frail platform, so loosely constructed that the eggs appear to be in danger of falling through the interstices.

On the other hand, the robin builds a bulky, compact, thick-walled nest of mud, reinforced with grass and straw. In contrast there is the dainty, trim nest of the ruby-throated hummingbird and the exquisite woven structure of the Baltimore or northern oriole, perhaps the finest example of avian architecture.

All kinds of materials are used by birds in nest building. Many birds, like the grasshopper and field sparrow, use grass. Others, such as the hawks and herons, build their nests of twigs and sticks. The red-eyed vireo uses strips of bark, bits of dead wood, paper, and the down of plants. The robin, as we have already remarked, uses mud as does the phoebe. The parula warbler weaves a nest of the usnea lichen already hanging from the tree limb.

Birds select the materials for their nests from among the things they generally come in contact with. They use only those materials that conform to the general type of nest characteristic of the species. Thus a certain chipping sparrow lined her nest with fine wire rather than the customary horsehair, and crested flycatchers sometimes pick up cellophane cigar wrappers as a substitute for cast snakeskins.

Not only do birds make use of a wide variety of materials, often displaying great ingenuity in nest building, but they also adapt themselves to varying or changing environmental conditions. The red-wing will build a much deeper nest in a place subjected to strong winds than in a sheltered location. The chimney swift now builds in our chimneys in preference to the hollow trees in which it formerly nested, and we find the phoebe and barn swallow making use of manmade structures whereas they originally built their nests on rocks.

Some birds, not satisfied that the sites they have selected

offer sufficient concealment for their nests, go to great lengths to further hide them or otherwise circumvent their enemies. The meadowlark and some sparrows arch over their nests with growing vegetation, and the ovenbird covers its nest with dry leaves from the forest floor where it nests, while the ruby-throated hummingbird and the wood pewee, which are unusually adept in the art of camouflage, cover their nests with lichens so that they appear to be excrescences on the branch of a tree.

Sometimes birds will depart from the general rule, both as to location and the materials used, in building their nests. Thus a blue jay was found building on a tree root projecting from an overhanging eroded bank instead of in the usual pine tree, and a hermit thrush built in a hole in a haystack instead of in the crevice of a rocky, wooded bank. And flickers have been known to drill their nesting holes through the outer walls of ice houses and deposit their eggs on the sawdust insulation between the outer and inner walls.

Most birds nest singly, but a few, like the purple martin and some of the swallows, herons, terns, and gulls, nest in colonies. The bobolink, the redwing, and the marsh wren, nest in somewhat scattered communities. As a rule, birds build their nests for only one season. A very few use the same nest year after year, though crows and hawks often rebuild their old ones.

Skunk
The friendly enemy

There was the summer's day when I was walking along a woodland path, and as I turned to follow a bend, I nearly walked into a skunk that was following the same path. Indeed, another step and I would have walked right into him. Needless to say I was brought up short. Not wanting to have an encounter with the animal, with perhaps disastrous results, I stood there without making the slightest movement or sound. Whether the animal knew I was there and preferred to ignore me or whether he was unaware of my presence, I don't know; in any event he continued on his way in his unhurried fashion and I watched him until he was out of sight. Then I waited a few more moments before I resumed my walk. I did not see him again, and I finally emerged from the woods onto the road that led to my home not too far away.

I am firmly convinced that the skunk is the most misunderstood of all our wild animals. We are, it seems, instinctively impelled to shy away from him as if he were some loathsome thing. The pity of it is that there is probably no animal more harmless and inoffensive than this little Ishmaelite of our fields and woodlands.

It is true, of course, that at times he does offend our sensibilities, but such occasions are rare. He resorts to his defensive weapon only when he senses his life to be in danger. At all other times he is exceedingly neat and fastidious in his personal habits, and he always minds his own business. Withal he is easy to look at. He likes the companionship of humans and, since he is of gentle disposition, can be easily domesticated; indeed, if taken when young, he will make an affectionate and entertaining pet, as tame and as playful as a kitten and far more intelligent and amusing. I do not think the skunk deserves the unpleasant notoriety that we have heaped upon him; I think we should accept him as a friend, which in truth he is.

Whatever our personal feelings may be toward the animal, we must admit that the skunk makes a striking appearance with his handsome coat of glistening black, set off with two broad white stripes, and his large and bushy tail, which he carries about like a flag. He cannot be called handsome, for his head is somewhat too long for his body and his snout far too pointed. His front legs, too, are very much shorter than his hind ones, giving him a very peculiar gait, but this feature doubtless serves him in some way.

The long claws with which his forefeet are armed are of practical value. He uses them to turn over stones in his search for insect food and to dig his burrow, although he frequently makes use of a rabbit or woodchuck hole, a small cavity among rocks, or a hollow log for a home.

The skunk is mainly nocturnal in habits but may be found quite frequently wandering about the woods and fields in broad daylight. He does, however, prefer to rest in his retreat during the day and as a rule does not leave it to forage for food until dusk has fallen. With the coming of night he awakens from his slumbers and becomes an active, nimble, little creature. I have often met him on moonlit nights while on his hunting excursions, the white of his stripes standing out quite brilliantly and giving warning that here is one it is best to leave alone.

His movements are quite deliberate and without haste, as if

he were aware of his immunity to attack. He is perfectly fearless of man and other animals and if left alone will continue on his way with a genteel and dignified indifference. But his immunity from attack has made him careless about profiting from experience and more than once has proved his undoing, for he has never learned to avoid a trap or the dangers of the highway.

As he ambles along, the skunk carries his tail at a slight elevation. The moment danger threatens, he raises it still higher so that the long hairs hang drooping like a great plume. Here is a conspicuous and unmistakable hint that the skunk will tolerate no fooling. If anyone, human or animal, fails to heed it, he quickly presents his rear and discharges the powerful effluvium for which he is so well known, at the same time arching his tail high above his back so that he himself will not be defiled.

The odorous fluid, which is stored in two glands located under the tail, is ejected by muscular contractions a distance of ten feet. It is yellow in color, somewhat phosphorescent, and resembles musk in its extraordinary volatility. It is also intensely acid, burns the skin like fire, and in extreme cases has been known to cause blindness. The discharge at any time is scarcely three drops, and yet this small quantity will pollute the air for half a mile or more in every direction. The mephitic odor holds terror to most animals and provides the skunk with immunity against attack, although he has been known to fall victim at times to the horned owl, fox, and bobcat.

The skunk's diet consists essentially of insects, small mammals such as mice, birds, mollusks, crayfish, and an occasional snake. He may occasionally pay a night visit to a chicken yard, but the harm he causes in his respect is more than balanced by his destruction of injurious rodents and noxious insects. As a matter of fact, farmers are rapidly learning that the skunk is a valuable ally in keeping down the population of farm pests, and in many states he is protected by law. As it should be.

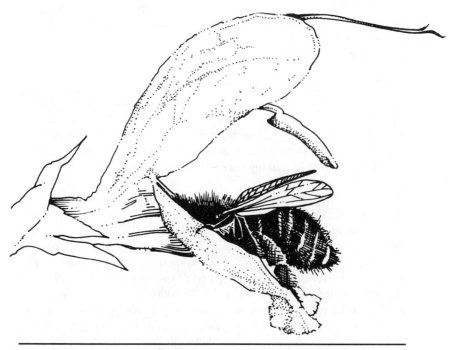

Honey Bee

A matter of conservation

As the departing summer and the approaching fall give evidence that the winter season is near at hand, the animals of the wild begin to make preparations for combating the low temperatures, the ice and snow, and the chilling winds of winter.

Some of them migrate to a warmer climate or seek some protective refuge; others go into hibernation to pass the winter in more or less a state of dormancy; many will remain active. But these animals, too, make adjustments: Thus the mammals put on their winter underwear in the form of very dense short hairs that sprout among the long true fur. The birds are protected in a similar manner: Their plumage is more dense and more closely interlocked than that which follows a spring molt. Ducks and related birds acquire a downy undergrowth that helps to keep out the cold.

The grouse grows fringes of sharp points on his toes to serve as snowshoes, and the varying hare not only puts on a white robe but also grows long, stiff hairs along the margins of his feet, permitting him to race with abandon over deep snow in which other animals would flounder. The invertebrates, too, take precautions against the winter cold, either by seeking refuge in some protected place or by constructing shelters of various kinds.

But there is one animal that can do none of these things— the honey bee. The honey bee cannot migrate because of its size and inability to fly long distances. Neither can it hibernate or remain about, for it cannot survive low temperatures. And so it has but one course open to it—to lay in a supply of heat-producing food and to create a thermal environment of its own.

As most of us know, a honey bee community consists of three castes: the queen, workers, and drones. The queen is the egg-laying member of the community whose sole function is to perpetuate the species. The workers, as their name implies, perform all the labors incidental to the maintenance of the community. Upon them devolve the duties of cleaning and repairing the hive; feeding the young, the drones, and the queen; guarding the hive; secreting the wax and building the comb; gathering pollen and nectar; and making and storing the honey.

The drones have but one purpose in life—to fertilize the queen. Apart from this function they are of no service, and their very name has become an expression for laziness. Moreover, they are as helpless as they are useless. Their tongues are not long enough to get nectar from the flowers, they haven't any baskets in which to carry pollen, they lack a sting with which to fight, and furthermore they haven't any pockets for secreting wax. Who is to blame the workers, then, if they begrudge the drones the honey on which they feed, particularly when the shortening days of autumn herald the approach of winter, and the flow of honey is almost over or has even come to an end.

Economy must now become the watchword in the hive, and with an instinctive thrift the workers place the drones on the debit side of the ledger. Now that their excuse for living is over, the drones have become a burden that might jeopardize the safety of the community, and so, without hesitation the workers drive them from the hive, fulfilling the law of nature that the useless must perish.

Having rid themselves of the drones, the workers begin their preparations for the winter. The queen ceases in her reproductive labors entirely, releasing the nurse bees from their duties of feeding the young, and the nectar hunters make fewer trips afield, venturing abroad only during the sunny hours of midday. The loads they carry become steadily lighter. It has been estimated that 480 pounds of honey are required to maintain an average-sized community throughout the year and that 17,760,000 trips are required to accumulate this amount. These countless journeyings represent an intense industry, and the surplus, stored in thousands of waxen cells, must not only carry the bees through the winter but must also provide for brood-rearing in the spring. We can understand, then, why the bees cannot be prodigal of such reserves and why they find it necessary to get rid of the drones.

But this hoarding instinct would, in itself, serve no useful purpose, if the bees were not able to generate and conserve heat. They are unable to survive temperatures below fifty-seven degrees Fahrenheit and would perish if they could not raise the temperature of their surroundings above this point. So in order to maintain a high enough temperature, they gather together into a single compact cluster inside of which they produce heat by muscular activity and which they leave only for nourishment or to make quick cleansing flights.

At first the bees do not form the cluster where the combs are filled with honey, for the sheets of honey separating them would make it difficult to conserve the heat. Instead, they form the cluster where the last brood emerged. Here they find empty cells in which to crawl and are separated only by thin walls of wax. As the cells are emptied, the bees shift the cluster so that they are always near a food supply. In early fall the cluster is usually low and near the entrance, if there is considerable honey stored. The movement is usually upward and toward the rear of the hive as winter progresses and food is consumed.

Since the purpose of the cluster is to conserve the heat generated within it, the size of the cluster varies with the outside temperature. On warm days the bees do not generate any heat and therefore do not have the need for a tight cluster, but as the temperature begins to fall the cluster becomes more and more compact, while at the same time the temperature inside increases rapidly.

This cluster consists of a hollow sphere of bees several layers thick and is an excellent nonconductor of heat. It is so effective that a point inside it may be one hundred degrees warmer than a point a few inches away and outside of it. Within the hollow are bees that move about freely, and it is these bees that generate heat by muscular activity, such as by movements of the legs and abdomen and especially by fanning their wings. The remaining bees are inactive and form the shell of the cluster, but they constantly shift their positions and exchange places with the bees within. The number of inactive bees varies with the temperature, being larger at warmer temperatures and smaller when more heat is required.

To maintain the necessary muscular activity, the bees are forced to draw upon their food reserves. The undigested material, which forms excreta, is retained in the hind intestine until the bees have an opportunity for flight, for normally feces are not deposited by the bees within the hive. During cold winters there are times when the bees cannot fly for weeks, and as the generation of heat during this period requires an increased consumption of food, the result is an increased amount of feces.

Field Cricket
The night serenaders

Leigh Hunt wrote of the cricket:

> *And you, little housekeeper, who class*
> *With those who think the candles come too soon,*
> *Loving the fire and with your tricksome tune*
> *Nick the glad silent moments as they pass.*

Hunt had in mind the house cricket, a species not native to America but which has become established here and is now widely distributed, though not abundant. Our own field cricket, however, also has a liking for warm corners and in the autumn frequently enters our dwellings. I have always found it a delightful occasion to have one of these merry little musicians of our fields pay me a visit and entertain me with his cheery chirping, though my wife is horrified at the thought of having them in the house because she claims they eat the rugs and other fabrics. But I have never found them to be destructive. My only regret is that when one comes into the house he does not remain for very long.

I have known people who were greatly annoyed by the chirping of crickets as they tried to go to sleep on a warm summer's night. But I have always found it restful to lie awake listening to their serenades until I gradually get drowsy and eventually fall asleep.

We all know the field cricket—the large black species common in the fields and in our gardens and backyards. Field crickets lurk beneath stones and other objects on the ground or burrow into the earth. They are for the most part nocturnal in habit, though they may be seen during the daytime. They usually feed on plants, such as clover but are sometimes predaceous. In captivity they will eat melon or other sweet, juicy fruits.

Field crickets are provided with two pairs of appendages called palpi—one situated above, the other beneath, the "chin"—with which they test the eating qualities of various substances. They move their jaws sideways instead of up and down, and it is most interesting to watch them bite out pieces from a blade of grass or a chunk of melon and chew it with apparent gusto. Also, when eating they take hold of the food with their front feet as if afraid someone might take it away from them.

Unlike the grasshoppers, to whom they are closely related, the crickets do not have any wings beneath their wing covers and therefore cannot fly. They are, however, good jumpers, their hind legs being long and muscular and capable of catapulting them through the air for quite a distance. But that is not the means they usually employ to escape their enemies. Their six legs are more suited for running, and if you should try to capture one, you will discover how fast it can move over the ground. They are very slippery, too, as you may also discover when you may think you have caught one—only to find it slipping through your fingers. You need but look at the patent-leather finish to their bodies to see why it is so difficult to hold on to them. Here we have an adaptation that permits them to slide more easily between blades of grass. It was doubtless acquired through eons of evolutionary processes.

Look at a few crickets closely, and you will probably find that some of them have what appears to be a tiny crowbar sticking out from the hind end of their bodies. This "crowbar" is a device for laying eggs and is found only in the females. They use it for making a hole in the ground in which to lay their eggs so that the eggs will be safely protected during the winter.

If you have never seen a cricket chirp, find a male—only the males chirp—and watch how he raises his wing covers to an angle of forty-five degrees and then rubs them rapidly together. If you want to know just how the wing covers produce a sound you will have to examine one of them with a magnifying glass or hand lens. You will observe that the veins form a peculiar scroll pattern, which serves as a framework for making a sounding board of the wing membrane by stretching it out like a drumhead. You will also observe near the base of the wing cover a heavy crossvein covered with transverse ridges—it is called a *file*—and on the inner edge of the same wing cover near the base you will see a hardened area known as the *scraper*. The cricket sounds his note by drawing the scraper of the underwing cover against the file of the overlapping one, an action that sets the wing covers into exceedingly rapid vibration. It is as if we drew a file across the edge of a tin can. The can is set to vibrating and thus makes a sound.

At this point we may well ask the question, why do crickets chirp in the first place? At one time it was believed that the male crickets chirp to attract the females. This view was discarded when it was found that the males often played their fiddles when there were no females around, and even if the females were present they paid little or no attention to a fiddling male. It is true that a female may wave her antennae in his direction, but she will also wave them at a stick or stone.

At any rate, we now know that when crickets chirp, they also produce notes too highly pitched to be audible to us. They use these ultrasonic notes to communicate with one another, the chirps being merely incidental. It has also been established that the field cricket has at least three basic sound signals: a calling note, an aggressive chirp, and a courtship song, which presupposes that the crickets can hear. Look on the tibia of each front leg and you will find a small, white, disklike spot. This is the auditory organ, or ear.

Winter Birds
Winter companions

Winter in New England can be rugged, but there are days when the sun shines brightly and the temperature is moderate. On such a day I was wandering afield and chanced upon a flock of goldfinches feeding in a field, which brought to mind the following words of Keats:

Sometimes goldfinches one by one will drop
From low-hung branches; little space they stop,
But sip, and twitter, and their feathers sleek,
Then off at once, as in a wanton freak;
Or perhaps to show their black and golden wings;
Pausing upon their yellow flutterings.

Although these birds are at their best in late summer or early fall, when they may be seen in flocks feeding upon thistle seeds, of which they are especially fond, they are always a delight to watch. In winter, for instance, they may take possession of some field and meticulously go over the weeds for the seeds that still remain on the dried and withered stalks.

Winter is the time of the year when most of us prefer to sit snug and complacent beside the warmth of the fireplace. But this is also the time of the year to get outdoors and become acquainted with the birds that have chosen to remain with us, braving the terrors of the season to cheer us with their companionship, and also to get acquainted with those that have come from more northern regions, to tarry with us until spring sends them back to their breeding grounds.

We forget the nip in the air and the snow on the ground that makes walking difficult when we glimpse among the naked branches of some tree a little mote of gray and white moving about with lively abandon. We can see the chickadee at all seasons, for he is with us the year round, but it is in the winter that we really notice him and learn to appreciate his presence. For when all nature seems to have retired before the icy blasts of the north wind, the chickadee is about, gay and happy, enlivening the winter scene with his amusing acrobatics and merry chatter of "chick-a-dee-dee-dee-dee." He actually seems to enjoy a snowstorm, and even in the most bitter weather we find him frolicking from tree to tree, laughing and joking in his own inimitable way. He is the bird of whom Emerson wrote:

> *This scrap of valor just for play*
> *Fronts the north wind in waistcoat gray,*
> *As if to shame my weak behavior.*

We frequently find a white-breasted nuthatch or two in company with the chickadees, for the two birds hunt together all winter. It is not a partnership—both working for mutual benefit—but rather an association due to similar tastes. Their food consists of beetles, caterpillars, and pupae of various insects, and these they search for among the cracks and crevices of trees. The chickadees hunt over the twigs and smaller branches, while the nuthatches confine themselves more to the trunks and bases of the branches.

The nuthatch is a most industrious little bird, always seeming to be on the move, climbing up or down the trunk of the tree with evident ease. He goes straight up or straight down or spirally around it, according to mood and moves so rapidly that he has earned the sobriquet of the "tree mouse." As the poet would have it

> *The busy nuthatch climbs his tree*
> *Around the great bole spirally,*
> *Peeping into wrinkles gay,*
> *Lazily piping one sharp note*
> *From his silver-mailed throat.*

As we wander about the countryside, we will most likely come upon a flock of juncos merrily chattering away in a clump of hemlocks. We may also find these birds in weedy and bush-grown fields, where they run over the ground or on the snow or perch upon shrubbery, the cold or whirling snow never seeming to bother them as long as they can find something to eat. And weedy fields where the brown stalks of weeds and grasses stand in phalanxes against the sky also provide happy hunting grounds for the tree sparrows, which we easily recognize by the black sepia blotch of their plain fluffy breasts. With cheerful, hardy industry they fly from one brown patch to another, clinging to the dead stalks as they carefully go over them and pick out the seeds.

Every now and then, one or more tree sparrows, made thrifty by the winter dearth, will descend upon the snow and hop around and search for seeds that have been scattered by the wind. It is not alone a serious quest for food that these birds engage in; to them it is also a frolic, if we might judge from the convivial notes that fall upon the air like the tinkling of sleigh bells.

Woodpeckers are always in evidence in the woods and orchards, and if we listen carefully we should hear them tapping as they search for insects hidden away in the trees. Then without warning, a flock of evening grosbeaks may suddenly appear from out of the sky and take possession of a roadside thicket to feed on the seeds and buds of various trees. And in almost any orchard we might expect to see a flock of cedar waxwings, seduced there no doubt by the frozen apples that still remain on the branches.

With the exception of one or two species, such as the snow bunting, which habitually seeks open fields far from all cover, most of our winter birds prefer sheltered places like thickets and bush-grown roadsides, stands of pine and other coniferous trees, orchards, and cedar or alder swamps. In alder swamps we may frequently come upon a flock of redpolls, fearless and usually friendly little birds but sometimes during the winter extremely wild.

Golden-crowned kinglets and brown creepers seem to prefer woods of oak and maple, while crossbills, pine grosbeaks, and pine siskins frequent stands of coniferous trees when these trees bear fruit. Myrtle warblers are very fond of bayberries, and where these berries are abundant we should expect to find these little birds with yellow rumps. Beneath a tangle of wild grapevines we might discover a ruffed grouse and perhaps startle the bird to taking flight with hysterical notes of alarm that would set a blue jay to screaming in the distance. In the words of Thoreau, "That unrelenting steel-cold scream, unmelted, that never flows into song, a sort of wintry trumpet, screaming cold, hard, tense, frozen music, like the winter sky itself."

For the song sparrow we must visit a swamp or marsh, and for the Ipswich sparrow and horned lark we must travel to the seashore. The crow, starling, and shrike are all birds of the open country. The screech owl prefers the orchard, especially if there is a hollow tree for shelter. How this smallest of our nocturnal birds of prey got his name I don't know. Certainly his cry is not a screech, but a singularly mournful and plaintive wail.

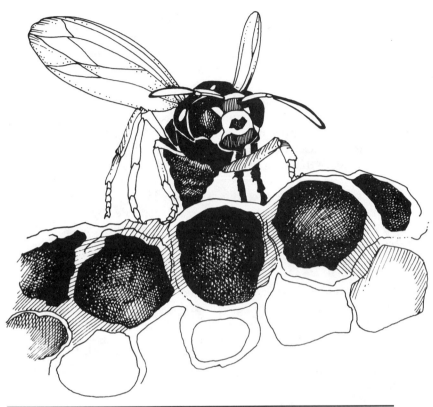

Paper Wasps
The paper makers

I am sometimes inclined to believe that all human activities, or at least many of them, have counterparts in the animal world. Consider, for instance, the manufacture of paper. The invention of paper making was fairly recent, perhaps a few hundred years or so ago, though the Egyptians were using papyrus on which to inscribe their records six thousand years ago, and even before that the Chinese used the bark from the mulberry tree for the same purpose. But certain wasps have been making paper for more years than we would care to count.

Wasps are irritable and nervous creatures at best, and it is wise to leave them alone. Most people are afraid of them, and well might they be, for some of them are quite formidable and can inflict severe wounds with their stings. However, species of the genus *Polistes* will tolerate our presence while in the process of building their nests, if we do not interfere with their activities, and will go about their business as if we were not there.

These *Polistes* wasps are quite common in our gardens and backyards in spring and summer and may easily be recognized by their brown color, folded wings, and slender abdomens. They build their nests in some secluded corner of the house or in the garage, a shed, or some other outbuilding and are familiar objects; most of us have seen them. One winter I counted thirty empty nests in my garage; they had not all been built the preceding summer, but represented wasp labor over several years. These open combs are suspended by a single pedicel to a corner of a roof, to the lower surface of a window ledge, or to the ceiling of a garage, barn, or shed. They are also found under rocks on the warm sides of ledges as well as in trees.

Unlike the ants and honeybees, wasps do not live in permanent communities. When cold weather sets in, ants pass into a state of dormancy, and honey bees cluster in their hive and remain semiactive, but in the case of the wasps, the entire community dies except the queens. This means that when spring returns, the ants and bees start in where they left off, whereas the wasps have to begin all over again. A new nest must be built and a family reared, which will endure for only a few months.

When the spring sun warms the earth, the queen wasps, which have spent the winter in some snug retreat, such as a crevice beneath bark or in a rotting log, emerge and begin to look about for suitable sites in which to build their nests. Having found a site, each queen starts her nest. First she scrapes some fibers of weather-worn wood from a fence, the side of an unpainted building, or some similar place and uses her jaws to make a paste by mixing the fibers with an oral secretion. She then builds a stalk, or pedicel, on the site that she has selected by depositing the paste little by little until it is about an inch or so long. On that she constructs a single naked horizontal comb, which resembles an open umbrella and contains several shallow cylindrical, cuplike cells.

Should we examine these nests sometime during the summer, we would find in some of them long, white eggs, in others chubby little soft-bodied grubs, and in still others pupae in various stages of transformation. The grubs hang head down and are held in place at first by a sticky disc at the rear end of their bodies and later by their enlarged heads, which completely fill the openings of the cells. They are constantly nursed by the workers that developed from the original batch of eggs and later by successive batches and are fed first upon the sugary nectar of flowers and the juices of fruits. Later they are given more substantial food, such as the softer parts of caterpillars, flies, bees, and other insects, which have been reduced to a pulp by mastication.

Toward the end of summer males and fertile females are produced, mating takes place, and young queens develop from the fertilized eggs. Then as cold weather sets in, the males and workers die, leaving the queens to find hibernating quarters, where they remain until the following spring. When they emerge, they build a new nest and rear a new family.

Most of us have heard of the yellow jackets, and many of us know them by sight. They are the small, trim black and yellow wasps that are common almost everywhere and often enter our gardens and back yards. They are formidable insects and will brook no interference with their activities, so it is prudent to give them a wide berth. Their nest consists of a series of horizontal combs suspended one below the other and all enclosed in a paper envelope, which is somewhat brownish in color. Some yellow jackets build their nest in a stump or beneath some object on the ground, but most of them build in a hole in the ground. I have often seen them in a hurrying, jostling throng going in and coming out of a hole that measured barely an inch in diameter. Some of them were returning from foraging expeditions and carried food; others were returning with loads of pulp made from wood fibers or partially decayed wood and were intent on adding it to the nest, which they gradually enlarge as the occasion demands. The wasps that were leaving carried pellets of earth, which they had scraped from the walls of the hole to make room for further additions to their home. None seemed bent on pleasure; they appeared, on the contrary, to be too busily engaged with their tasks to pay any attention to me, though doubtless they were aware of my presence

The extremely large paper nests we often find suspended from the branch of a tree or shrub are made by the bald-faced hornets, black wasps with a white face. They are similar to those of the yellow jackets but they are larger, of course, and the paper is a different color. It is of much stronger quality, too. In fact these nests are so strong that they endure well into winter, in spite of being buffeted by rain, sleet, and wind.

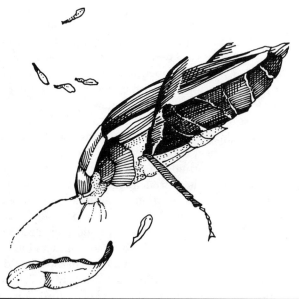

Diving Beetle
The ogre of the pond

Some years ago—in fact many years ago—an American entomologist by the name of Harris kept a diving beetle "three and a half years in perfect health, in a glass vessel filled with water, and supported by morsels of raw meat." I don't know what he attempted to prove by the experiment, if anything, but I would say he was guilty of cruel and abusive treatment in view of the fact that diving beetles are normally occupants of ponds and streams, where they can swim about in the far reaches of the water.

The diving beetles are abundant in our ponds and streams. If you should stand at the water's edge, you will likely see them hanging head downward from the surface of quiet waters with the top of their abdomen at the surface and the tips of their wing covers sticking out of the water, thus permitting them to breathe the upper air. Just before they dive, they lift their wing covers and take in a supply of air in the space beneath. They use this air to breath while submerged, and when it eventually becomes impure, the beetles rise to the surface, expel it, and take in a fresh supply.

The diving beetles are well adapted for an aquatic existence, having an oval body, which lessens water resistance, and long, flattened hind legs that serve admirably as propelling organs. The beetles are usually black or brownish, somewhat shiny, and marked with yellow. They have slender antennae, actually threadlike in form, in contrast to the club-shaped antennae of the water scavenger beetles with which they might be confused. The two resemble each other in general appearance. In some species, the males have little cuplike suckers on their forelegs, which serve as clasping organs while mating, and in some species the females exhibit in interesting dimorphism in that some of them have furrowed wing covers while others have smooth wing covers.

Some diving beetles are an inch and a half long while others are minute. But big or little, and in either case quite innocent looking, they are fierce and voracious and a terror to the other small inhabitants of the ponds and streams. They not only feed on other aquatic insects but attack all sorts of other animals, including snails, mussels, tadpoles, salamanders, and even small fishes. But the diving beetles, in turn, are not immune to attack by other animals, such as ducks (teals, the wood duck, mallard, and pintail), frogs, salamanders, turtles, and fishes, in spite of the fact that they can emit a fluid from glands located at the front and after ends of the body that is supposed to be distasteful to potential enemies.

The diving beetles may be seen throughout the warmer months. They spend the winter in the bottom mud of the ponds and streams or beneath the banks, where they remain in a dormant or semidormant state except when they are attracted to the surface by a rise in temperature. I have particularly liked visiting a woodland pool during a February thaw to watch them swim about in the water. They can be seen to best advantage at this time, for the water is fairly clear, not filled with submerged vegetation and debris.

The diving beetles are able to fly and often fly from one pond to another. Being attracted to lights, they are frequently seen flying around our porch lights at night or around street lights. Many species, and there are quite a few of them, are able to make sounds, either by rubbing the abdominal segments upon the wing covers or by rubbing the hind legs upon a rough spot on the lower side of the abdomen.

The larvae, or young, of the diving beetles are as ferocious as the adults and even more bloodthirsty. They are queer-looking animals, elongated and spindle shaped, with large oval or rounded heads that are flattened and large sickle-shaped mandibles. Each mandible has a groove on the inner side, which serves as a passageway for the body juices that the larvae suck from their victims—instead of devouring them whole, as the adults do. They also inject a digestive juice into their prey that converts the body tissues into a liquid form.

The larvae, popularly known as water tigers because of their predaceous habits, swim about in a rather leisurely manner. The legs are the chief means of propulsion, but a larva can also make a sudden spring by throwing its body into serpentine curves. For the most part, however, the larvae creep about on the bottom mud or on submerged leaves to which they cling when resting or when lying in ambush. Long hairs on the last two abdominal segments and two small appendages at the tip of the abdomen help them to cling to the surface film while they are in the process of obtaining air. And what might appear to be rather strange is that although both the larvae and adults are aquatic, the pupal period is passed inside a cell in the soil or in an earthen cell under a stone or log on land, well away from water.

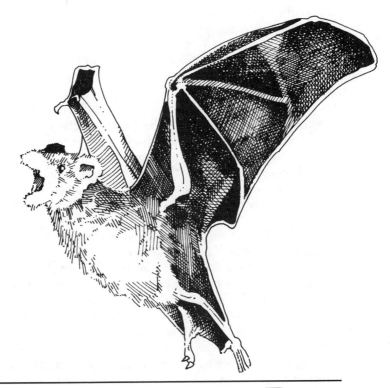

Bats

The demons of the night

We generally dislike bats because of their mouselike appearance and the silly superstitions that many of us still accept. Many of us, too, fear these demons of the night, as they have been called, because of the stories we have read about bloodsuckers or vampires. But vampires inhabit the tropics, and so we are not likely to meet them unless we visit such places. As a matter of fact, the bats are bright, engaging little animals, and the superstitions that link them with evil do them a grave injustice.

Bats occur all over the world and vary in size from the mouselike species to the big "flying foxes" of the Malay region whose wings may measure as much as thirty inches from tip to tip. The large bats are fruit eaters, but the majority, including all our eastern American bats, are insectivorous and feed on the wing.

It may seem odd to some of us, but bats are true mammals though they have, in some ways, the habits of birds. From their flight we might well suppose that their wings are like those of the birds, but actually they are quite different. They are more like a duck's foot, consisting of a membrane stretched between elongated fingers. This membrane is thin but very tough and leatherlike and extends from the sides of the body to the ends of the hands and feet and back to the top of the bony tail, so that the animal has a winged margin all around its body. The feet are provided with claws, and at the top of the wing the thumb projects in the form of a very serviceable hook, which they use to drag themselves along flat surfaces or for scratching the backs of their heads.

The bats are adapted almost entirely for flight and are not all fitted for walking. Their legs are twisted around in such a way that their knees bend backward in a direction different from ours (as the arms do also), which makes it exceedingly difficult for them to walk. When they attempt to do so, they succeed in only a flapping shuffle.

There are many species of bats in the United States, but one of the most widely distributed and most common is the little brown bat. We may find this species almost everywhere but especially about towns and villages. Shortly before dusk, it leaves its daylight retreat—behind a shutter or in a loose piece of bark, the recesses of a cave, or the attic of a house—and launches forth upon its nightly flight, perhaps heading first for some nearby pond for a drink before setting out to break its fast.

The bat's flight is swift and erratic. Watching the animal speed through the air, darting here and there with incredible swiftness and making sharp turns without visible effort, we are amazed at its agility, which even the swallows and swifts cannot match. Its uncanny ability to fly among the branches of trees at terrific speed without hitting any of them is likewise amazing. I have many times waited with breathless expectancy for it to crash into some object for which it seemed headed only to see it veer off suddenly to one side.

As everyone knows by now bats avoid obstacles and find their way about by echolocation, that is, they emit supersonic notes and hear the sound waves as they are reflected back. The membrane that serves as wings is equipped with sensitive nerves that respond to the reflected sound waves. By localizing the source of the reflected waves, the animals are able to locate an obstruction and thus avoid it.

While the insectivorous bats obtain their food on the wing, they do not do so in the same manner as the birds. They use the membrane as a collecting net, doubling it up like an apron, and either remove their victims with their strong teeth or fly to a nearby tree where they can manage the larger victims with greater facility.

The wings of the little brown bat often measure nine inches from tip to tip. Yet when folded, they hardly show because the bat does not fold them like a fan but draws them close to its body as one would close an umbrella. When the animal sleeps or rests, it hangs head downward, holding on to a support by means of the claws on its hind feet, apparently not at all inconvenienced by the rush of blood to its brain.

Unfortunately, whoever coined the phrase "blind as a bat" did not know his bats. Though the eyes of bats are small, they can see well enough. They appear keen and observant and quite in keeping with the alert attitude of the erect ears.

Artists of a past age fashioned their demons after the bat and had much to do with the way many of us regard this animal. Yet a look at its face, with its pug nose, and the sparkle of its mischievous eyes peering out from beneath the woolly eyebrows, and its wide-open pink bag of a mouth, we get the impression of impishness rather than of malignancy—and why not? For it is one of the most gentle and friendly of living animals. It seeks the shelter of our buildings, and on warm summer nights when flying abroad it seems fond of our society, though perhaps in all truth that may be because of the mosquitoes present.

Our bats are highly beneficial and destroy vast quantities of noxious insects. Such fears that they get into ladies' hair and bring bedbugs into the house are without foundation. Bats are very particular about their personal cleanliness and take great pains to keep their face and body clean, washing their face with the front part of their wings and then cleaning the wings with their tongue. After that they scratch the back of the head with their feet and then lick them.

Bird Migration
The perpetual mystery

I am still inclined to think that the most impressive sight I have ever seen was the time when I first saw a flock of Canada Geese flying overhead in their customary V-formation on their way to their wintering grounds. It was a beautiful autumn day, as I recall, cool and crisp, the blue cloudless sky hanging like a canopy over the painted landscape and the fragrance of burning leaves pervading the air. And as I watched with awe as the birds soared across the sky to disappear in the distance, I wondered what it would be like to take wing and fly to some distant place.

Today we need only to step into a modern air liner to have such dreams come true, but somehow I cannot get as much of a thrill in flying as I might have experienced if in my youthful fancy I could have stepped on a magic carpet and followed the birds to wherever they might have gone.

When we see the geese on their way southward, the migratory flights are in full swing. During the months of July and August most birds are not too much in evidence, but with the coming of September they reappear in the open to gorge themselves on ripening seeds and fruits in preparation for their journeyings. A few have already departed. In the early morning we can observe the ducks moving toward the coast to spend the winter in the salt marshes. Later in the day we might see the neatly uniformed redwings wheel and advance in military platoons over the marsh; on the morrow they will be gone. And we will also see the woodland birds flitting from thicket to thicket. They scud quickly to shelter as the ominous form of a hawk appears overhead, for now that the mating season is over, the hawks may frequently be seen sailing and gyrating high in the air.

Not all birds migrate by day. Go out on some moonlit night, and you may see hundreds of birds flying across the bright face of the moon, at heights of a quarter of a mile or so; or go out on a dark and misty night, and you will hear them calling to one another in an effort to keep together as they grope their way over the tree tops. My sympathy goes out to these invisible travelers as they hurry through the night, braving unknown terrors until morning dawns. Then they can feed and rest until night, to resume their hurried flight to the still verdant vegetation of the tropics some thousands of miles away.

It is still something of a perpetual mystery how birds find their way, especially when they strike out over a body of water such as the Gulf of Mexico or fly through the densest fog, and unerringly arrive at their destination. Every year scarlet tanagers cross the gulf, a distance of from five hundred to seven hundred miles, and bobolinks, black-billed and yellow-billed cuckoos, bank swallows, vireos, kingbirds, and others fly the five hundred-mile stretch of ocean between Jamaica and South America without anything to guide them but their sense of direction.

As for flying through a fog, we have the classic demonstration recorded by members of the biological survey attached to the Harriman Expedition in Alaska during the summer of 1899. The steamer bearing the party was enroute from Unalaska to Bogoslof Island, a distance of about sixty miles, and was making its way slowly and carefully through a fog so dense that objects could not be seen at a distance of three hundred feet. When the steamer was about halfway across, flocks of murres, returning to their nests on Bogoslof after a long search for food, suddenly appeared out of the fog wall astern and, flying parallel to the vessel, disappeared in the mists ahead. The ship was headed directly toward the island with the aid of a compass and chart, but its course was no more exact than that taken by the birds.

How well this sense of direction is developed in birds is shown by species in which the immature birds and adults migrate at different times. The belief still persists, I know, that young birds are first led over a route by older, experienced birds and that they thereafter regularly follow such a course year after year by memory and sight. This is doubtless true in some species, but it does not apply to those in which the young migrate at a different time. The young of such species apparently possess an inherited migratory instinct and a sense of direction; they instinctively follow more or less the same course as that taken by the adults, though they have never been over it before.

Amazing as is their sense of direction, perhaps even more astonishing is the faculty that many birds have of returning to the same nesting area. Many birds, including robins, bluebirds, and house wrens, often return to the same nesting site year after year, and I have known of a pair of bluebirds that returned to the same birdhouse in an apple orchard several years running. Strangely enough, the offspring rarely return to their natal area. It appears that they must first have nested in some particular area—the choice of their first nesting site being more or less a matter of chance—before they will return to it. A general exception to the rule is to be found, however, in most or all of the species that live in colonies. The reason would seem to be that they are more or less gregarious throughout the year and also perhaps that in some species, at least, the character of their habitat requirements imposes a definite limitation on nesting sites.

The distances some of the migratory birds travel each year seem almost incomprehensible when we consider their size and the difficulties and hazards they encounter on their flights. Scarlet tanagers that nest in Canada and New England migrate to Peru, and bobolinks, purple martins, cliff swallows, barn swallows, and some thrushes that spend the summer with us winter in Brazil. To the blackpoll warblers that nest in Alaska, such flights must seem a mere jaunt, for these birds travel to northern South America, some five thousand miles from their summer homes. The nighthawk, however, puts all land birds to shame when it comes to long-distance flights, for this bird migrates from the Yukon seven thousand miles south to faraway Argentina.

The migratory flight of the nighthawk is exceeded by many

water birds and, more notably, by some of the shore birds. There are nineteen species of shore birds that breed north of the Arctic Circle, and every one of them visits South America in winter, six of them penetrating to Patagonia, a migration route of more than eight thousand miles. When we see the small and seemingly frail hummingbirds about our garden flowers in spring and summer, little do we realize that they can and do fly five hundred miles across the Gulf of Mexico. If you think this is a record nonstop flight, consider the golden plover, which makes a twenty-four-hundred-mile nonstop flight from Nova Scotia to South America, a jump requiring probably forty-eight hours of continuous flying and a feat accomplished with the consumption of less than two ounces of fuel in the form of body fat. But of our migratory birds, the champion of them all is no doubt the Arctic tern, whose nesting and wintering ranges are some eleven thousand miles apart. As the route is circuitous, the tern probably flies at least twenty-five thousand miles each year.

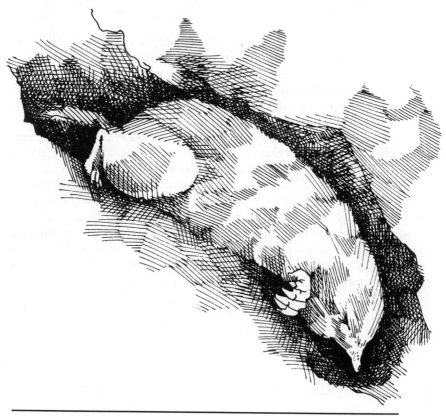

Mole
Dweller in darkness

Nature must have been in a petulant mood, to put it compassionately, when she designed the mole—destined to live in darkness and to dig always for its food in order to stay alive. Not an enviable existence, to be sure, and yet I am not too certain that such an existence does not have its compensations. For this little animal always has an abundance of food at its disposal—though it has to work for it, as all animals do—it is always sheltered from the elements, and it is relatively free from attack by potential enemies.

    Few of us see the mole, but we frequently find evidence of its presence in the ridges of upturned earth that so disfigure our lawns, damage our golf courses, and ruin the seed beds in our gardens and nurseries. These ridges, which indicate the direction and course of the mole's hunting paths, are not molehills but merely a raising of the sod or soil crust and are the result of the animal's tunneling too near the surface. The molehills, on the other hand, indicate deeper tunneling and are formed of earth pushed up from lower workings where the soil is too compact to be simply pushed aside.

The mole digs its tunnels at a depth varying from one or two inches to four or five, although when the ground is dry or when cold weather sets in, it may go down as much as ten inches. Apparently it digs wherever fancy or food takes it without thought of any definite plan, so that ultimately it ends up with an intricate system of many-branched tunnels. Those which it uses as permanent runways and for hunting purposes are as a rule constructed near the surface and along fences, hedges, walks, and plant rows, for such spots are less apt to be disturbed by man. Galleries or passages join the subsurface runs with the deeper runways, and here and there enlargements are made, one or more of which may be used during the breeding season for nesting purposes.

In excavating its subsurface tunnels, the mole uses its forepaws much as we would use our hands in swimming the breast stroke. They are brought forward until they almost touch in front of the animal's nose, then thrust outward and backward by the powerful shoulder muscles, thus pushing the earth aside. At the same time, the hind legs shove the body forward through the passageway thus formed.

Looking at the mole, we would expect the animal to be rather slow and somewhat methodical in its movements. But surprisingly, the speed with which it can tunnel through the earth is almost incredible. For instance, a mole has been recorded as having tunneled a distance of 225 feet in a single night. There is no denying, of course, that the mole is well equipped for digging. We have only to look at his greatly enlarged forelegs, which are provided with long, broad nails and an extra sickle-shaped bone on the outside, to realize what effective chisels they are for digging in the earth.

As a matter of fact, the mole is eminently suited for a subterranean existence. His head, for instance, is wedge-shaped, thus offering a minimum of resistance, and is set so close to the shoulders that there is virtually no neck. Both head and what there is of a neck, moreover, are provided with heavy muscles and are thus capable of a powerful upward heave. The body is cylindrical, which facilitates movement through the narrow passageways, and is further provided with ribs strongly braced to withstand pressure. Even the fur has been designed for an underground environment. It is a compact velvety coat that will lie either front or back with equal ease and thus relieve any friction from the walls of the tunnels, no matter which way the animal might travel.

Living in a world of darkness, the mole has little use for eyes, which are therefore underdeveloped and not much larger than a pinhead. Probably their only function is to distinguish between light and darkness. The ears are also small but nevertheless highly sensitive to sound waves and vibrations passing through the ground. The sense of touch is also highly developed. Both the snout and tail have numerous nerve endings, which guide the animal in going forward and backward.

The mole appears to be forever active and snatches its sleep whenever it feels the need although the common belief is that it works at regular periods each day. Even during the winter, when many animals are dormant, the mole continues to be active, but it seeks shelter deeper in the ground. The animal, however, is most active when soil conditions are favorable—after a heavy rain in summer or during a thaw in winter—for then the earth is easy to excavate. It is at such times that the mole usually extends its near-surface runs. At other times it uses its runs to go in search of food or when it must work in places unaffected by drought or frost.

The mole has an insatiable appetite and will eat most of its weight in a day. Such an appetite is undoubtedly due to the strenuous and active life it leads; indeed, it is doubtful if any other wild mammal does as much work in a day. It is exceptionally fond of earthworms but is also partial to white grubs, various beetles and their larvae, and a multitude of other ground-inhabiting insects such as centipedes and spiders.

The mole cannot go very long without food and will quickly die of starvation. In an experiment, a mole was given a pint of earthworms at 8 p.m. and no further food. By morning it was very feeble and cold and soon died. On examination, the stomach was found to be empty, although the animal had eaten every worm.

Living a secluded existence and sheltered from many of the dangers that threaten animals living above the ground, the mole does not have to produce a large number of offspring to maintain its kind. Accordingly there is but one litter a year.

The mole is relatively free from predation for several reasons: Its tunnels are so small that no formidable enemy, except perhaps small weasels and snakes, can follow it. As it rarely leaves its subterranean home for a visit above ground, it is not apt to be seen by other predators. Its peculiar rank odor is objectionable to some, if not all, potential enemies, and other animals find its soft, dense fur distasteful.

Woodpeckers
The tree tappers

We can hear the tapping of the woodpeckers throughout a year, as they search for insects in the trunks and branches of the trees. But it is in the winter that their tapping is most noticeable. Not only does the cold, crisp air serve as a sort of sounding board, but there are fewer other sounds to compete with the tapping. In the warmer seasons, we hear other birds giving voice to their calls and melodies and countless insects that buzz, hum, and chirp.

It is something of a mystery how the woodpeckers can unerringly drill into the burrow occupied by an insect beneath the bark or in the wood of a tree. There are some who believe that the vibrations produced by a grub as it cuts away the wood with its strong jaws are picked up by the beak and conveyed by the beak and skull to the brain of the woodpecker, but this does not explain how the bird can locate small grubs that make no audible sound, or grubs and ants that lie dormant and motionless in the winter. Perhaps it can fix the exact location of the burrow by tapping with its beak in somewhat the same manner that a carpenter, by striking the wall of a room with a hammer, can determine the position of a timber or stud hidden under laths and plaster.

The woodpeckers are familiar birds, and yet few of us realize how eminently successful they have been in competition with other birds. Long ago they discovered that by laying their eggs in hollow trees or cavities that they excavated themselves, their eggs would have better protection against the elements and various enemies than if they were laid directly on the ground or in some comparatively frail basket made of twigs, grasses, or similar materials.

But even before this discovery, the woodpeckers had become so modified in form and structure as to be assured of a constant supply of food in the form of insects that are to be found at all times of the year in burrows and beneath the bark of trees. Thus, while most birds must be content with such insects as they can find on the surface of plants or flying in the air, or with such seeds and berries as they can find on various plants, the woodpeckers are able by their physical makeup to find food at any time merely with the expenditure of a little energy.

The woodpecker has short, stout legs with two toes in front and two in back, furnished with strong, sharp claws. They are equally well adapted for clinging to the bark and for climbing. A further aid in helping the bird to maintain its hold on the trunk of a tree is its tail. It is composed of stiff feathers terminating in sharp spines or quills, which can be pressed against the bark and, acting like a wire brush, serve as a prop or brace to support it in an upright position while the bird is at work. Indeed, the woodpecker is better equipped for climbing than a telephone lineman.

All such equipment would be useless if the woodpecker did not have the means of penetrating the wood and dislodging the insects hidden there. And as remarkable as its climbing equipment may be, even more so are the tools with which it drills into the wood and extracts its food. Observe a woodpecker at work sometime (through a pair of field glasses if possible) and you will see that it draws its head and body as far back as possible and then strikes with all its might, sending its chisel-like beak, an exceptionally effective wood-cutting instrument, deep into the wood of the tree. We would think that such constant hammering of beak and head against the tree would produce concussion of the brain or some other injury. But the skull is thick and hard and otherwise so constructed as to be springy and jar absorbing.

But more remarkable still is the tongue, which is the most highly specialized organ of the woodpecker. It is very long and cylindrical, the tip hard as horn, with many strong barbs and with bones that are provided with a marvelous mechanism. This mechanism stretches the tongue, which normally lies soft in the mouth when not in use, beyond the tip of the beak and turns it into a highly effective instrument for spearing or dislodging the insects from their burrows in the wood or bark—a weapon more effective in its way than a fish spear.

The woodpeckers have come in for a lot of undeserved criticism. When we see these birds scrambling over a fruit tree or find their holes in the bark, we naturally come to the conclusion that they are highly destructive. But the fact is they rarely disfigure a healthy tree. The reason is that the woodpecker rarely has to penetrate far into a live tree for borers since most species that infest live trees are found just under the bark or in the sapwood not very far from the surface.

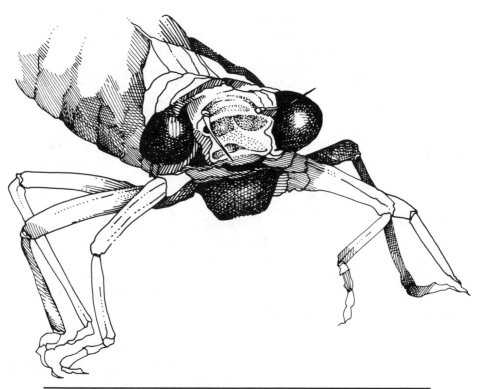

Dragonflies
The master aerialists

Although the natural habitat of the dragonflies is the pond or stream, these insects occasionally enter our back yard or garden. Some species habitually leave their normal water realm to fly about the countryside.

We used to know the dragonflies more popularly as the darning needles because they were said to sew up the eyes and ears of naughty children. How such a belief ever had its inception I'll never know, for the insects lack equipment to sew anything up, let alone being able to puncture the skin. But in a more credulous and superstitious age, all kinds of absurd notions found acceptance, and so we have several more myths concerning these insects: It was once believed that dragonflies could bring dead snakes back to life and were known as snake doctors and snake feeders. They were also known as horse sting-

ers and flying adders. But the dragonflies have weathered such slan-
derous epithets and today are regarded more favorably, especially by
those of us who know them well. For not only are they entirely harmless, but they are of considerable usefulness in controlling various insect pests such as mosquitoes. Hence they have come to be known as
mosquito hawks.

The dragonflies are conspicuous members of the water
realm and on a summer's day may be seen flying about the shores of our
ponds, lakes, and streams, soaring overhead, swooping over the water,
or hovering along the shore. We consider the swallows as masters of
flight, but some dragonflies equal these birds in speed and even exceed
them in agility. They are superb flyers, as they have to be, for they
depend on their wings for getting a living.

If we should watch these most attractive and interesting
insects closely, we would observe that some of them—the larger and
stronger ones—keep to the higher regions above the water, coursing
back and forth, passing and repassing the same point at intervals of a
few minutes, while the smaller species are less constantly on the wing,
usually flying in short sallies from one resting place to another or
hovering above the water before they alight. We would also observe
that some of them appear to patrol a regular beat, stopping at the same
places like watchmen at their time clocks. And as we watch them
darting here and there, now alighting on a water plant to rest a moment, now streaking off in pursuit of some other flying insect, we
might see one of them skim the surface of the water, then suddenly
swoop down and touch it. Or we might see another, momentarily
poised in the air, descend to the surface in a swift curving movement,
hover above a submerged leaf of a water plant, and then fly quickly
upward, only to descend again to the submerged leaf. Or we might see
a third alight on the stem of an emergent water plant rather near the
surface of the water and curve its body below it. These three dragonflies are merely following their own behavioral patterns, for all are
females laying their eggs.

The giant dragonflies are exceptionally powerful flyers and
despite their size have surprising agility. If you want to test your
quickness of eye and powers of muscular coordination, try to catch one
on the wing with an insect net—you will find that it is not easy. These
dragonflies roam far from the water and even dash into our houses
occasionally. They have a great deal of curiosity and will often remain
in one spot, their wings whirring so rapidly as to be only a blur, while
they examine some object that has excited their attention.

Looking at one of the larger dragonflies, some having a

wingspread of over seven inches, we can well understand why people of another time regarded them as fearsome creatures, for truth to tell, some of them appear quite ferocious. Their large heads and enormous bulging eyes are in themselves enough to frighten anyone timid and superstitious, but they serve the insects well, having become thus modified for their predatory mode of existence. The eyes, which often occupy the greater part of the head, each contain from twenty to thirty thousand facets, each facet representing the outer face of a visual unit. In many instances some of the facets are larger than the others, the larger ones presumably being able to distinguish objects seen from below and to the sides, the smaller ones detecting movement. And we must add that the head is able to rotate freely on a slender neck, providing the insects with a large field of vision.

The dragonflies, both in body form and structure, are admirably modified for the life they lead. Their mouthparts are adapted for eating prey; their thorax is thick and packed with powerful muscles to operate the wings; their abdomen is long, slender, and more or less cylindrical, well designed to permit the insects to move through the air swiftly and easily; and their legs are long and spiny and are placed near the front of the thorax. Moreover the legs all curve forward and are designed for grasping prey. In flight they are held basketlike, the better to capture flying insects, especially the midges and mosquitoes on which they feed. They are also adapted for grasping a twig or some other object on which the dragonflies may rest. The victims are often consumed in flight, but frequently the dragonflies will alight on some perch and eat them at leisure.

Finally, the dragonflies' wings are designed for the maximum in flight. As a rule, the forewings and hind wings are of similar size and structure and are tapered much like those of an airplane. They consist of a parchmentlike, or cellophanelike, membrane supported by numerous veins and, unlike those of other insects, do not move up and down in unison but beat alternately. Thus, while the forewings move upward, the hind wings move downward, the movement of the wings being so timed that the hind wings encounter an undisturbed column of air rather than the turbulence of air created by the forewings. The result is that both the forewings and hind wings meet a smoothly streamlined flow of air. All of which makes for a very efficient flight.

Jumping Spiders
The jumpers

We usually associate spiders with webs and rightly so, for they do spin webs, which we find during the warmer months in fields and meadows and on our lawns and throughout the year in our houses. And then there is the famous Scottish story of Bruce and the spider.

But not all spiders spin webs. There are, for instance, the wolf spiders, which capture their prey by stalking it or chasing it over the ground in the manner of wolves; hence their name. There are the long-legged brown spiders that may be seen, especially in spring and early summer before the ground vegetation has become too thick and profuse, running through the grass, over woodland paths, and along fence rails. Then there are the crab spiders, so named because they resemble crabs, that lie in ambush in flowers and in secluded places on the ground until some unfortunate victim comes near. Then they pounce upon it. And then there are the small or medium-sized spiders that are known as the jumping spiders, and with good reason. They actually jump—contrary to what we may expect of spiders. They jump from bush to bush, from stem to stem, and often considerable distances for such small animals, as much as forty or more times their body length.

Watching these jumping spiders, we are amazed at the ease and seeming abandon with which they leap. And should they miss the perch for which they aim, they do not plummet to the ground, as we might expect. They save themselves with strands of silk that they spin and attach to the support from which they leap. Since the strands are also attached to their bodies, the spiders are prevented from falling should they fail to reach their intended landing spot. The spiders also use the strands to climb back to their takeoff spot, should they wish to return to it. These strands of silk are collectively called the dragline and are spun by the spiders wherever they go. Not only does the dragline serve as a bridge from one place to another but it also provides the spiders with a means of escape when pursued or threatened by an enemy, such as a predator. Jumping spiders have often been seen under such circumstances to jump from a cliff or from the side of a building and then to float down to safety on their dragline.

Like the wolf spiders, the jumping spiders are also hunters and are quite common on plants, logs, fences, the sides of buildings, and similar places, where they attract our attention by their short, stout bodies, rather short, stout legs, conspicuous eyes, bright colors, and more particularly by their quick jumping movements. The body, as a rule, is thickly covered with hairs or scales, and their front legs are thicker than the others, in the males being bedecked with conspicuous plumes and ornaments that are used during the courtship rituals. It is rather surprising to find that the hind legs, which are most used in jumping are neither modified nor strengthened as they are in such animals as the frogs and kangaroos. Possibly the small size and weight of the spiders do not warrant any modification of the hind legs. The sexes differ little in size but often differ greatly in color and in their hairs and scales.

The jumping spiders are keen-eyed hunters, stalking and attacking insects with a precision and alertness that is astonishing. They can move forward, sideways, or backward with equal facility and hunt during the daytime. They are the friendliest little animals. Sometimes they will sit on your finger and observe every movement with an attention not usually seen in other arthropods, limited as they are by complex instinctive behavior patterns. Their keen eyesight enables them to detect movements at a distance. On spying their prey, they creep forward until they are close to it, when they suddenly and quickly jump on it.

The jumping spiders do not spin webs, but they do spin retreats in crevices, under stones on the ground, under bark, and on plants. The retreats are saclike in form, made of thick, white, slightly viscid silk of several layers, and are usually provided with two openings. Many spiders retire into these retreats at night and during cold days and also use them when molting and for passing the winter as juveniles or hibernating adults. The females also lay their eggs in them, usually in spring and summer.

The jumping spiders are most ardent in their love making, particularly the males, which put on a display that compares favorably with the courtship antics of many larger animals. At mating time the males of some species will dance before the female and strike the most singular postures, holding their legs extended or sideways or over their heads in such a way as to show off their ornaments, or moving them about to attract attention.

George William Peckham, the American entomologist, has given us a charming account of the courtship of a pair of these spiders each of which was only one-sixth of an inch long. He writes:

> *When some four inches from her, the male stood still, and then began the most remarkable performance that an amorous male could offer to an admiring female. She eyed him eagerly, changing her position from time to time, so that he might always be in view.*
>
> *He, raising his whole body on one side by straightening out the legs and lowering it on the other by folding the first two pairs up and under, leaned so far over as to be in danger of losing his balance, which he only maintained by sidling rapidly towards the lowered side. . . . Again and again he circles from side to side, she gazing toward him in a softer mood, evidently admiring the grace of his antics. This is repeated until we have counted 111 circles made by the ardent little male. Now he approaches nearer and nearer, and when almost within reach*

whirls madly around and around her, she joining with him in a giddy maze. Again he falls back and resumes his semicircular motions, with his body tilted over; she, all excitement, lowers her head and raises her body so that it is almost vertical; both draw nearer and nearer; she moves slowly under him, he crawling over her head, and mating is accomplished.

Salamanders
The fire monsters

There was the time when a neighbor called and asked me to come over to his house and identify an animal that he had found in one of his window wells. I found the animal in question to be a spotted salamander, which was not surprising, for the animal often takes to wandering about the countryside, though its normal habitat is the moist woodlands. It will appear in the most unexpected places: window wells, cellars of city houses, gardens, and on mountain slopes high above the nearest pond or slow-moving stream.

In ancient times, *salamander* was the name given to a mythical lizardlike monster that was able to live in fire and quench it by the chill of its body. Pliny in his *Natural History* refers to it, but it was

Paracelsus, the famous alchemist, who named the imaginary creature. Salamanders, of course, cannot live in fire, nor can any other animals. Nor are salamanders lizards, as becomes quite obvious when a salamander and a lizard are compared. A salamander has a soft, moist skin, whereas the skin of a lizard is covered with scales.

I have often thought the spotted salamander to be a rather handsome animal. Yellow spots adorn the glistening upper blue-black surface and the lower half of the sides, and the lower surface is a dusky slate flecked with white. It is largely nocturnal in habits, spending the day beneath a log or stone or lying buried in the soil, emerging when the sun has set to feed on earthworms, snails, slugs, millipedes, centipedes, spiders, and insects.

In the fall the spotted salamander may sometimes be seen abroad during the day, and there are records of its having been seen crawling over the snow in winter. But such winter appearances, at least in the northern part of its range, are unusual. As the weather becomes colder, the animal seeks a winter refuge beneath a rotting log, under a stump, or in a hole in the upper layers of the woodland leaf cover, where it remains until the following spring.

The spotted salamander reappears in March or April, according to locality, and as soon as the weather permits, it starts out for the nearest pond or quiet inlet of a stream, where it will breed. It travels only at night, only when the temperature is above the freezing point, and only when it is raining or has rained during the day, though it may be stimulated to travel by a rapid run-off of snow following a decided rise in temperature.

How the salamander can locate water at some distance from its winter quarters may appear to be something of a mystery, but it is no mystery at all. The animal locates water by showing a positive response to gravity (positive geotropism). As it moves downhill, it is sensitive to a moisture gradient in the air and heads for conditions of increasing moisture.

As a rule, the male salamanders arrive at the breeding place a day or two before the females. Some ponds may contain hundreds of salamanders, and when they engage in a sort of nuptial dance, the scene becomes most spectacular and is worth observing. They swim around, over, and under one another, rubbing and nuzzling together so vigorously in their excitement as to make the water fairly boil. Every now and then they break the surface to take in air, adding to the illusion of the bubbling water.

Following the courtship dance, the males deposit their spermatophores on submerged leaves or stems of water plants. The spermatophores are vase-shaped masses of clear jelly that have a flattened flangelike base and are capped with a white woolly substance. They look much like glass push pins and contain hundreds of spermatozoa. After the spermatophores have been deposited, the females crawl over them and take them into their cloacal chambers. There the spermatozoa fertilize the eggs, which are then laid. They hatch within two or three weeks into greenish yellow or greenish brown slender larvae, which remain in the ponds until they are mature, in late summer or early fall, and then move onto land as spotted salamanders.

In early spring most of our amphibians, that is, the frogs, toads, and salamanders, emerge from the places where they have spent the winter and migrate to the ponds and streams to mate and lay their eggs—with one exception: the red-backed salamander.

This salamander is a small species, measuring not much more than three inches in length, with a slender body and of a uniform plum red color or often red with a light stripe down its back. It is more adapted to life on land than most salamanders, and it is less dependent on water. We usually find it in the woods, more frequently in damp or moist woodlands. It also occurs in comparatively dry places but only if there is access to a source of moisture through a burrow or crevice.

The red-backed salamander is a very secretive and timid little animal and nocturnal in habits, hiding by day beneath moss, bark, logs, and stones. When revealed in its hiding place, it rarely attempts an immediate escape but remains quietly curled in the position in which it is found. Touch or prod it, however, and it will usually run off, though *run* may not seem quite the word to use. Its legs are relatively weak and must be aided by looping movements of the tail so that the animal appears to progress over the ground by a series of rapidly executed leaps.

Sometimes we find specimens with partly regenerated tails, and occasionally when we overturn a stone or log, we may find a portion of a tail wriggling violently. The animal has the ability to cast off part of its tail at will, which is a sort of protective device, for an enemy bent on its capture would be first attracted to the violent movements of the detached part of the tail, thus giving the salamander a chance to escape.

Unlike the spotted salamander and the red-backed salamander, which seek winter quarters on the approach of cold weather, the two-lined salamander may be seen in almost any brook at any time throughout the year, even in winter. A saturated area near a spring or seep is also a favorite habitat.

This species is among the smallest of our salamanders, measuring from 2½ to 2¾ inches in length, though sometimes they are as long as four inches. Its color varies from a dull greenish yellow to bright orange yellow and brown and is most in evidence on the back in a broad median band and on the lower surface, where bright yellow predominates. The median band is usually peppered with small black spots that may unite to form a narrow median dark line. On each side of the band there is a dark line, gray, brown, or black, that extends from the eye along the trunk and tail. This color pattern serves to distinguish this salamander from other species.

The two-lined salamander is essentially a brookside species. It hides beneath all kinds of objects at the water's edge, and we can find it by overturning stones or logs and all manner of rubbish. It is an extremely active salamander and when alarmed or disturbed escapes into the water so rapidly that we are hardly aware of seeing it. It does not depend entirely on its diminutive legs to effect its escape but succeeds in promoting its rapid progress by doubling its body into a series of wavelike movements and then suddenly straightening it, the result being a number of bewildering jumps. Once in the water, it hides beneath the stones. During warm weather it may wander about on land, and if we do not live too far from its natural habitat, may venture into our garden or back yard.

After a brief courtship, the female lays her eggs, which vary from white to pale yellow and are variable in size. They hatch into exceedingly slender larvae that measure about half an inch long. They have a distinctive gray or slightly brownish pigment, arranged in a netlike pattern on a light yellowish or slightly greenish yellow ground. This greenish yellow ground is mostly confined to the trunk. Flecks of dark pigment are also scattered throughout the light band that runs along the back. On each side of this band there is another band that encloses a series of six to nine, but usually seven, definite light spots.

The change to the adult form is very slow, and it may take two years or longer before the transformation is fully complete. The larvae stay in much the same places as the adult salamanders and, like them, dash out in a flash when disturbed. Both live mainly on water insects and worms, though they also feed on spiders and sowbugs.

Fox
The master of wile

No longer does the howl of the wolf, conveying its eerie sense of peril, startle the lonely settler in his woodland cabin, but we still hear the fox as he barks at night from a glistening hilltop.

The beauty, natural grace, and intelligence of the fox commend the animal to everyone; I doubt if any animal has made a greater impact on legend and literature or has received greater attention for artists of every genre. We all recall Aesop's fable of the fox and the grapes, perhaps the best known of his fox fables, and some of us may also recall Grimm's story of the fox and the wolf.

But undoubtedly the best known of all literary accounts of the fox is the medieval beast epic satirizing contemporary life and events. It is found in French, Dutch, Flemish, and German literature and is known in France as *Roman de Renart*. The English version is *Reynard the Fox*, which is Caxton's form of the name in his translation (from the Dutch) published in 1479 as his *Historie of Renyart the Foxe.*

A glance at the dictionary will also show to what extent the word fox has become part of our vocabulary. As a noun it is used to denote a sly, cunning fellow and a rope yarn and in combination with another word to describe a kind of dog, the fox terrier, a kind of grass, the foxtail, and a kind of dance, the fox trot; the adjective *foxy* means "wily," and the verb *to fox* means "to trick" and "to discolor (prints and books) with a stain."

All of the above is evidence of how highly people have come to regard this doglike animal of the wild and to admire his personal qualities of shrewdness and cunning, his boldness and audacity, as well as his caution, and above all else his well-developed intellect. This last quality is manifested in the way he learns from watching humans and profits by such experience, thus avoiding the many dangers that beset him on all sides. Instead of escaping into the wild, he has chosen to match his wits with those of the trapper and farmer, and in spite of continued persecution, he has been able to maintain himself and even increase in numbers. Indeed, he may live for years in a thickly settled area and even within the limits of a great metropolitan city.

The fox is such a well-known animal that he hardly needs description. He is doglike in general appearance, about the size of a small collie, with a pointed nose, large triangular ears, and a bushy tail. The upper parts are a rich golden reddish yellow, the underparts and tip of the tail white, and the feet black. The color, however, varies with the seasons; in the winter the fur is full and lustrous, in the summer faded and pale, and relatively short. Various color phases occur as black, silver, and cross or patch, but whatever the color phase, the tip of the tail is always white.

The fox is an animal of diverse habitats. Though he prefers the rolling farm land with its sparsely wooded areas, streams, and marshes, he may also be found along the borders and in the open areas of forested regions. He is essentially nocturnal in habits but may also be seen in the fields and meadows, during the day, hunting mice which in the winter appear to be his staple food. One reason for his survival is his varied diet: he will eat almost anything, plant or animal, dead or alive. When the snow cover is deep in the winter and his usual food is scarce, he will take to eating the dried grass stems that tower above the snow.

His travels during the winter cover a greater range than in

summer. At this time of the year he is not so bound to his den as during the warmer months. He will sleep in any protected place, where he will curl up in the snow with his bushy tail across his nose and feet and benefit by the warmth that it provides. But his bushy tail may also be a hindrance if it becomes heavy and bedraggled with snow and sleet when he is being pursued by an enemy bent on his destruction.

Those of us who live in the country have often heard the thin, querulous barking of the fox on a still winter's night. It is not an attractive sound, but much less appealing is the weird scream of the male fox—probably the most sinister, unearthly wild animal note that can be heard in North America.

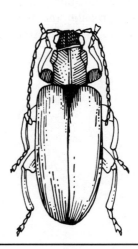

Leaf Miners

The miners

Should we be of an observant nature, we would notice that as the summer progresses, the leaves of various plants become disfigured by white or grayish blotches or twisting lines. If we are also of an inquiring mind, we might well wonder what caused this change. If we hold such a leaf up to the light, we may see that the blotch or twisting line is occupied by a tiny, wormlike creature. On the other hand, the animal that made the marks may have reached maturity and transformed into an adult insect, when it would have left its temporary home and taken up a different kind of existence.

The blotches or twisting lines are passages or tunnels that the larvae of certain insects excavate in the tissues of the leaves as they feed on them. The insects may be beetles, flies, moths, or sawflies, and since the passageways are called mines, the insects are known as leaf miners. Despite their diversity they all have one feature in common—small size.

It seems incredible that some insects are so small that they are able to live between the upper and lower surfaces of a leaf that is almost of paper thickness. But not only can they live there; they manage to grow and increase in size. This is indicated by the increasing width of the passageways. Follow one of them from the beginning and note that it begins almost as a pinpoint—here is where the egg hatched—and becomes progressively wider and wider.

I have always wondered if James Russell Lowell had these leaf miners in mind when he wrote:

And there's never a leaf nor blade too mean
to be some happy creature's palace.

Whether such creatures are happy is a moot question, but since they are provided with plenty of food and have a shelter over their heads, we may take the poet's word for it. Anyway the patterns these insects describe in the leaves are as varied as the insects themselves, and as each species makes its own characteristic mine, anyone familiar with these insects can usually identify the species by merely looking at it. Indeed, as one writer has put it, "They write their signatures in the leaves."

Some mines are long, narrow, and more or less winding. They are known as linear mines and are typical of the moths. A few mines are very narrow at the beginning and gradually enlarge, frequently terminating in a blotch suggesting a head. Such mines are termed serpentinic and are common on nasturtium and columbine. Others, called trumpet mines, also start from a narrow beginning but enlarge more rapidly and extend in a more or less regular curve, an excellent example being that made by the trumpet leaf miner of the apple. Still others are mere disclike blotches. These are referred to as blotch mines and are characteristic of the leaf-mining beetles, flies, and sawflies. Some mines are found immediately beneath the upper surface, while others are nearer the lower surface. The position of the mine is determined by the nature of the feeding. Thus species that feed upon the palisade cells are visible only from the upper side; those that feed on the parenchyma are visible only from the lower side of the leaf. On the other hand, species that eat both the parenchyma and palisade cells are visible from both sides. There are, moreover, many modifications of the two general types of mine, that is, the linear and blotch. The modifications include the linear blotch, the trumpet, the digitate, and the tentiform.

The leaf-mining larvae are usually flat in form and without legs; if legs are present, they are very small. Some larvae also have a wedge-shaped head for separating the two epidermal layers of the leaf as they move forward. Their jaws are usually sharp and are provided with powerful muscles, but in the sap-feeding species the mandibles are platelike, with many sharp teeth adapted for cutting through the plant cells and causing the sap to flow. In some species the larvae feed only on the sap, in others upon the cells. The sap-feeders are usually linear miners; the blotch miners are for the most part cell eaters. There are even some species that start out as sap feeders and end up as cell feeders.

The larvae of some leaf miners spend their entire larval existence in the leaf. Others feed in the leaf only for a time and then emerge and feed externally. Some have even developed the habit of entering new leaves when their food supply is exhausted or when the leaves in which they are mining wilt or become undesirable for further occupation. When the times comes for pupation, or transforming into the adult form, the miner may emerge and transform elsewhere rather than remaining in the leaf to pupate. Indeed, the behavior of the leaf miners is far from constant; their habits vary considerably. Thus, those that pupate in the leaf may have a naked pupa that rattles like a seed within the dried walls, or they may attach the pupa to the interior surface of the mine with silk or by some other means. Some even spin silken cocoons.

Despite having plenty of food and shelter at their disposal, the leaf miners do not live an altogether carefree existence. Sometimes they find the veins of the leaves a barrier to further progress, and they must cut through them or confine their operations to a limited area. They must be careful, too, not to cut the latex cells lest secretions pour out from the walls and drown the animals. But the gravest problem is waste disposal.

Some species have solved the problem by distributing their wastes over the floor of the mine; others excavate side chambers in which to dispose of them, and still others cut holes in the surface of the leaf through which they expel them.

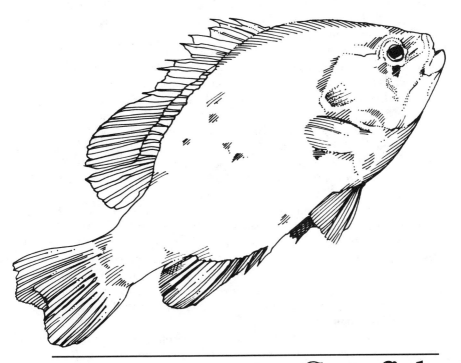

Sunfish
The incomparable

It seems to be a trait of human nature to assume that the best things come from distant lands. In our search for the rare and exotic, we are likely to overlook many interesting things close at hand. The goldfish that ornament our library table or grace our outdoor pool, originally came from far away, and the delicate tropicals that so delight the amateur aquarists come from the four corners of the world. But in our own ponds and streams are many handsome fishes with interesting habits, and yet how many of us know about them. I have often wondered why more of our amateur aquarists have not made a hobby of them, for they are easily managed, are tenacious of life, and are a source of perpetual enjoyment.

The sunfish! I still thrill to the name. It brings back memories of another day—the summertime, a small boy, and a homemade fishing rod. And how that small boy, flushed with excitement, found joy in matching his skill with this gamy little fish.

The sunfish, so named because it loves the sunshine and is more or less retiring when the sky is overcast, occurs in clear brooks and ponds and is a most beautiful animal. Perhaps you might not think so should you see him from above or in the bank shadows, for then he appears a drab olive, but let him swim out in the sunshine, and you will find that his sides are a rich iridescent blue and green flecked with orange and dimly barred with olive. There is no mistaking the sunfish, for near the edge of the gill cover is a bright scarlet spot, and if looked at from the side, resembles a pumpkin seed. And so we also know it by the name of pumpkin seed.

The male sunfish is more handsomely marked than the female and during the breeding season, in late May or June, his colors are even more pronounced. He puts these colors to good use, exhibiting them before some lady sunfish with all the vanity of a peacock. Indeed, if we are lucky enough to find him in the act of courtship, we will observe his strutting before his lady love with his gill covers puffed out, the scarlet spot standing out bravely, and his black ventral fins spread wide to show their patent-leather finish.

Should he succeed in winning the one for whom he has performed so valiantly, he invites her to the nest that he has already, in optimistic expectancy, prepared. This nest is a saucerlike basin, perhaps a foot across and several inches deep, which the male has excavated near the shore. Usually it is in a mass of dense vegetation, but not so dense as to exclude the heat and light of the sun. Strange as it may seem, the sunfish excavates the nest by fanning the gravel away with his tail and pulling the heavier stones with his mouth.

On reaching the nest, the male and his bride begin to swim around in circles with their ventral sides close together. While swimming, the female deposits her eggs, which fall to the bottom and become attached to the small pebbles forming the nest bed. The male at the same time discharges his sperm into the water. Their marriage is a short-lived affair. Soon after the female has deposited her eggs, she swims away, leaving her husband to guard and attend them, a task that he faithfully performs. After the eggs have hatched, he also swims away, leaving his progeny to take care of themselves as best they can.

As I write, the following lines from Longfellow's *Song of Hiawatha* come to mind:

Slowly upward, wavering, gleaming
Rose the Ugudwash the Sunfish;
Seized the line of Hiawatha
Swung with all his weight upon it.
. . . .
But when Hiawatha saw him
Slowly rising through the water,
Lifting up his disc refulgent,
Loud he shouted in derision
Esa! esa! shame upon you,
You are Ugudwash, the Sunfish;
You are not the fish I wanted;
You are not the King of Fishes!

Perhaps it is true that the sunfish is not the king of fishes, but try to convince the young angler of it. For the sunfish, the incomparable, has always been the small boy's fish, and through the years no fish has brought more joy to the American boy. Let us hope it will continue so.

Toad

The gardener's best friend

Few animals have been so maligned as the toad. The superstitions of the middle ages ascribed all sorts of evils to the animal, and unfortunately many of them still persist. But in reality the toad is a most useful animal, a great boon to the gardener, and altogether harmless; he is no threat to anyone except the animals on which he feeds.

Why do you think he has taken to living in our gardens? Simply because he finds an abundance of food there. He may not have as much intelligence as some other animals, but he is wise in many ways. For instance, he sleeps during the greater part of the day partly because he doesn't like the heat of the sun and partly to escape his various enemies. But as the sun begins to sink in the western sky, he comes out from some snug retreat and begins his nightly hunt through the garden and over the lawns in search of food.

The hunt is always an exciting one, for the toad eats only living, moving food, and since he has an enormous appetite, he must hunt almost incessantly to get as much as he needs. He is well equipped for catching the kind of food he eats because the tongue with which he captures his prey is attached to the front of his mouth instead of the back and can thus be extended fully two inches in an exceedingly rapid movement. Moreover, it has a sticky surface from which the escape of his prey is virtually impossible.

To watch a toad eat is well worth a few moments of any-one's time. Observe how still he sits, his head bent slightly forward, his eyes bright and intelligent. A fly alights within two inches of his nose. His mouth opens, and the fly is gone. So quickly does he thrust out his tongue, to which the fly adheres, and conveys it to the back of his mouth that we are hardly aware of what has happened.

The toad will eat almost any small living animal that is abroad in late afternoon and at night. Flies, beetles, grubs, caterpillars, crickets, grasshoppers, tree hoppers, ants, plant lice, army worms, spiders, sow bugs, earthworms—all are included in his dietary. It has been found that about 88 percent of a toad's food consists of insects and other small creatures that are considered pests in the garden. It has been estimated that in three months, a toad will eat some ten thousand injurious insects, and of this number 16 percent are cutworms, 9 percent caterpillars, and 19 percent weevils and other injurious beetles.

Some years ago these statistics were evaluated in terms of dollars and cents. It was found that at that time a toad was worth $19.44 in a single season because of the cutworms alone that he devours. In these inflationary days we might well wonder what a toad is worth. Moreover, a toad is especially valuable in greenhouses, which it will clean of slugs, snails, cutworms, and injurious beetles as well as sow bugs, which eat the roots of all kinds of plants.

I have yet to understand why people in general have an antipathy toward toads or experience a feeling of revulsion on seeing one of these animals. Perhaps one reason is that the toads live in dark, damp places and are therefore loathsome. Another is that toads are supposed to be cold and slimy to the touch. And still another is the belief that they cause warts.

It is true that toads select cool, moist places in which to stay when not out hunting for food because such places provide not only shelter but also moisture. A toad does not drink in the ordinary way but absorbs water through his skin. Keep a toad in a dry place, and he soon gets thin and becomes distressed looking; if not given access to moisture within a few days, he will die. But let him have plenty of moisture and he will remain plump and contented, even though he might not get much to eat.

Now just because a toad does not drink in the usual manner, we must not get the idea that he does not enjoy drinking—if we can use such a word. Observe sometime how he sprawls out in shallow water or on a wet surface and with what evident enjoyment he literally soaks in the water.

A toad is often cold to the touch but at other times can be quite warm. The reason is that the temperature of a toad's body changes with that of his environment. Unlike humans, who are only partially dependent on the sun for warmth, the toad is wholly dependent on it. On a warm, sunny day he might be very warm indeed and, conversely, on a cold day very cold, so cold in fact that he might dig down in the earth and sleep all day.

As for being slimy, the toad is not slimy at all; on the contrary he is very dry. Of course, should you squeeze him a little too hard or handle him somewhat roughly, he will become slightly wet, but this is his way of informing you that you are hurting him; it is his defense against enemies. The fluid that he pours out at such times is colorless and quite harmless.

But the toad has another fluid, which he secretes when he is in great agony and which is slightly poisonous. This fluid is secreted by the skin and is especially abundant in the paratoid glands, the two large swellings behind the eyes. The toad usually reserves this means of defense for times when he is seized by the teeth of an enemy, for the fluid has a disagreeable effect on the mucous membrane of the mouth. I have seen more than one dog drop a toad in a hurry. This fluid, too, is harmless to humans unless it gets in the mouth or eyes. The belief that either of these fluids causes warts is pure nonsense.

The toad is not without a certain beauty. Examine one closely if you will, and look especially at the eyes. I think you will find them both brilliant and beautiful, in fact so beautiful that they gave rise in past ages to the fable of the "jewel" in the toad's head. This jewel was supposed to be a precious stone within the toad's head and when worn as a talisman was believed to protect the wearer from all sorts of evil. It was Shakespeare who wrote:

> *Sweet are uses of adversity,*
> *Which like a toad, ugly and venomous,*
> *Wears yet a precious jewel in his head.*

Shakespeare, of course, was wrong on two counts.

The general color pattern of the toad is somewhat variable. In the summer it is usually dull brown, but very often the ground color may be yellowish brown. There is usually a line of a lighter shade down the middle of the back, and the wartlike elevations may be tipped with red, although above the ears they are often of a bright orange hue. Frequently there are four larger elevations or spots of color arranged along each side of the line in the middle of the back. They may be bright red brown conspicuously bordered with black, the black in turn being ringed with yellow, producing the effect of yellow-rimmed eyes.

This is not brilliant coloring, perhaps, but it is utilitarian. The toad's dull brown skin, rough with warts of all sizes and shapes, is so like the soil of garden and field that he becomes inconspicuous to his enemies. His size and shape tend to make him look like a stone or a lump of earth. Then, too, he has the ability to change the color of his coat. Among green foliage he becomes conspicuously spotted and striped, so that he blends with the lights and shadows of the grasses and leaves about him.

Gray Squirrel
The cacher

I daresay that of all our wild mammals none is better known than the gray squirrel. We find him in almost every municipal park, of whatever size; he is an occasional or frequent visitor to our garden or back yard, depending on where we live; and he is a common inhabitant of our woodlands.

I could never really understand why some people dislike the gray squirrel and regard him as a nuisance. It is true that he will visit the feeding stations that we set out for the birds and that he will occasionally pilfer an ear or two of corn. And it is also true that his gnawing habits and his tendency to rob birds' nests are points against him. Yet it seems to me that no one could help but take a liking to the bright-eyed, frisky little animal. I have always found him responsive to my overtures of friendship and have long since discovered that I might find a few moments of surcease from the cares and worries of the day's work in his companionship. If you have ever had one of these little gray beggars climb over your coat and take a nut or two from your hand you know what I mean.

The gray squirrel is not a fair-weather friend, and if you treat him right he will always be near at hand. Several of them are daily visitors to my grounds, scampering over the lawn and nibbling on a piece of bread or some other delicacy that I have put out for them, then chasing one another up a tree. At times I watched one run along a telephone wire with all the aplomb of a professional tight-wire walker, his bushy tail serving as a balancer. I have never seen one fall.

Even during the winter, the gray squirrel is up and around, except during a severe storm, when he will retire to his home until it passes. As he does not hibernate, he does not have to lay up large quantities of food to see him through the winter, being confident that he can find what he needs by diligent search. He has, however, in common with other squirrels, the habit of digging holes and caching a nut here and there for future use. I have often watched him bury nuts and have been deeply impressed with the seriousness with which he goes about his task.

The next time you find a squirrel so engaged, stop and watch him for a few minutes. Observe how he presses the earth firmly in place with his front paws after he has dropped a nut in the hole and refilled it with loose earth. Observe, too, how careful he is not to leave any trace of his excavating. Before he goes off to hide another nut, he covers the spot with loose grass and leaves.

At one time it was believed that this habit of burying nuts was merely an idle pastime, for it seemed impossible that nuts concealed in so many places could ever be recovered. Yet it is far from an idle pastime, for the squirrels can locate these nuts weeks later, even when the ground is covered with snow. I have frequently seen them during the winter as they sniff about on top of the snow, then suddenly stop and start digging, to come up with a nut a few minutes later.

The hidden nuts do not wholly sustain the squirrel during the winter. He must scurry about to find other food, such as the nuts that still persist on various trees. Of course, he is not the only claimant for such nuts and must compete with the red squirrels and the red-headed woodpeckers. The woodpeckers seem to think that the nuts are exclusively theirs and enforce their rights with their sharp bills. The red squirrels, too, resent competition from their larger relative and will not hesitate to attack him.

Whether the gray squirrel is an arrant coward or simply prefers to live in peace, I do not know; at any rate he usually retires upon the appearance of a red squirrel. With such keen competition to meet, it does not seem as if the gray squirrel would succeed in getting many nuts, but he has solved the problem by rising early and getting to them before the others arrive.

The gray squirrel is something of a plutocrat. Not satisfied with having a winter home, he must have a summer one also. His winter, or real, home is in the hollow of a tree, usually a maple, birch, or beech, with the entrance forty to sixty feet above the ground. His summer home is an outside affair and is built high among the branches. It is made chiefly of sticks, bark, and leaves, with a lining of grasses or some other material.

Perhaps you have seen these nests and have thought them to be crows' nests, as they are much alike in appearance. The squirrel's nest is bulkier, however, and contains more dead leaves, with an entrance on the side. Just why the squirrel builds a second home is not known. Perhaps he finds such a home cooler in the summer, or possibly he builds it as a pleasure house, just as some of us have camps in the mountains or cottages at the seashore.

Should food become scarce in his locality, the gray squirrel will figuratively pack up and go in search of a better neighborhood. Sometimes a number of them will get together and move a considerable distance. Years ago, when squirrels were far more numerous than they are now, mass movements involving countless numbers occurred every now and then. Natural and artificial barriers meant nothing to them, and without hesitation they swam lakes and rivers. In 1933, for instance, a thousand or more squirrels crossed the Connecticut River in one day and three months later were seen crossing the Hudson River.

A number of legends are associated with these earlier migrations, one having it that when the squirrels came to a river bank, they dragged large pieces of bark into the water and, climbing onto them, raised their bushy tails and were wafted to the other shore. A delightful story.

Unlike his cousin of the country and woodlands, the gray squirrel of our cities and towns has become, through his association with people, so tame and confiding that he will readily come up to you if you have something to offer him. Stroll through any park and one of these little gray beggars will invariably "hold you up" with a mute appeal in his eyes for something to eat.

Do not ignore his request if you have his well-being at heart and especially during the winter. The nuts he has hidden will not be enough to see him through, and he must find other food, as nut-bearing trees are not too plentiful in the city. In this respect he is not so fortunate as his country cousin. But do not, in mistaken kindness, offer him peanuts. Peanuts are unnatural animal food and have an ill effect on squirrels, making them sick and mangy and their fur thin and ragged.

Snakes
Snakes alive

Most of us object to snakes, and many of us are actually afraid of them as well we might be, for some of them are dangerous. However, most snakes are quite harmless, and some of them are actually beneficial. Indeed, when you get to know some of the more familiar species you may well wonder why so many of us dislike them. Take the brown snake for instance.

The brown snake is a most inoffensive animal and so secretive in its habits that it may venture right into our back yards and gardens without our even being aware of it. It is rather common in vacant lots, where it hides under trash of all kinds, especially old linoleum and roofing. In more natural surroundings, such as swamps, woods, and hillsides, it hides under loose stones or flat rocks and logs and bark most of the day, coming out late in the afternoon to search for food. It feeds essentially on snails and slugs but also eats earthworms and various kinds of insect larvae.

The brown snake, which might almost be called the city snake because it often turns up in parks, cemeteries, and vacant lots, is a small species seldom exceeding twelve inches in length and is rather drab in color. It is chestnut or grayish brown with a clay-colored stripe down the middle of its back, bordered more or less with small black spots. The abdomen is pinkish white.

Snakes have the habit of continually flicking their tongue in and out, as anyone who has watched a live snake knows. The movements of the tongue hold a peculiar fascination for many people, particularly those who are afraid of snakes and know little about them. Perhaps people regard the tongue as an offensive weapon, a sort of stinging organ. Actually the tongue helps the snake to smell.

The sense of smell, as a matter of fact, is well developed in snakes, and many species depend on odor to locate their food. Odor plays an important part in mating, also, and in many species enables the sexes to locate each other. This is particularly true of the brown snake. During the mating season the female secretes a strong odor from the skin and from glands in the base of the tail. This leaves a trail that the males can easily follow.

I know of no reptile, or any other wild animal for that matter, more gentle or docile than the green or grass snake. Never have I been able to induce one to bite, and even when newly captured it will submit to the most vigorous handling without showing the slightest sign of anger. Open fields and fence rows are this snake's normal habitats. It usually stays on the ground, crawling slowly through the grass, though occasionally it climbs into bushes and vines, where it coils itself among the stems and tendrils. A beautiful green, it blends so well with its surroundings that it is usually found only by chance. One time when examining some tangles, I found one twined about a stem, but I question if I would have seen it had it not moved when I inadvertently rubbed against it. It is fond of crawling beneath flat stones that have been warmed by the sun; if discovered in such a place, it will escape into the surrounding vegetation with bewildering speed. Once in the vegetation, it will perceptibly slacken its pace as if aware of the protection afforded by its color.

Ever since man saw his first snake, serpents have had the most curious effect on the popular imagination. Hence it is not strange that these animals through the ages have been invested with all sorts of odd behavior. Even today there is widespread misinformation concerning them, for instance, the rather fanciful tale that snakes swallow their young to protect them when alarmed or molested.

The snake most commonly believed to do so is the garter snake. This snake is one of the few serpents that bear its young alive, and I rather suspect that the manner in which it gives birth to its young is responsible for the story. Many persons get so excited on seeing a snake that they are quite incapable of accurate or critical observations; their reports are more or less based on hallucinations in which they see what is in their minds. Thus a person who does not know that some snakes give birth to living young might easily conclude that the babies have been swallowed.

The story is absurd, of course. The simple fact is that if snakes swallowed their young to protect them, there would have to be some way of temporarily turning off the excessively active digestive juices—and this they cannot do.

The garter snake is our most common serpent and is the most generally distributed and abundant of our harmless snakes. It occurs in almost every kind of environment, is fond of both dry and damp situations, and is at home equally in a bog, marsh, field, or pasture, as well as in our garden and back yard. The garter snake is not a particularly large snake, an extremely large specimen measuring only about three feet in length. It varies in color but in general has three yellowish or greenish stripes against a ground color of brown, green, or black, usually with a double row of alternating black spots between the stripes. A sun-loving species, it may often be encountered in the sun in an open space as we stroll along a country road or follow some woodland path. In early March, even though patches of snow still remained on the ground, I have often come upon hundreds of garter snakes in an open sandy area getting the full benefit of the sun. But then as soon as the sun begins to sink in the western sky, they return to their winter shelter among the clefts and fissures of some rocky site. All of which reminds me of the following:

> *A chipmunk, or a sudden-whirring quail,*
>   *Is startled by my step, as on I fare,*
> *A garter snake across the dusty trail,*
>   *Glances and—is not there.*

Equally as preposterous as the belief that snakes swallow their young is the milk snake story, which has almost assumed the proportions of a myth. Once upon a time, so the story goes, some misguided farmer, unable in any other way to account for the failure of his cows to give their normal quota of milk, found a scapegoat in the milk snake simply because he had seen the snake in the same pasture as his cows. On such flimsy evidence was the snake convicted of stealing milk.

It is true that the milk snake, a rather slender, strongly blotched serpent, may at times be seen in a pasture, but it is more likely to be found in open woods and around barns and stables and not necessarily around barns in which cows are kept. Moreover, it is a secretive species and is seldom abroad during the day, preferring to prowl at night and to remain hidden during the daylight hours beneath flat stones, the bark of rotting logs or stumps, boards, and other cover. And though it is also true that snakes will at times drink milk, they will do so only if water is unavailable. What is more, a full-grown snake would ordinarily not drink more than two teaspoonfuls of water at one time. He would be an unusual farmer, indeed, who could detect this small difference in the amount of milk produced by a cow at milking time. Furthermore, as the milk snake has several rows of needlelike teeth, it is inconceivable that any cow would permit a snake to fasten itself to her teats. And the fact remains that no one has ever seen the milk snake or any other snake suck milk from a cow. What is more important is that the milk snake feeds primarily on mice and rats and hence is of considerable value in keeping these rodents under control.

That snakes can swallow prey several times larger than themselves may come as a bit of surprise to those who do not know too much about snakes. As a matter of fact, they can not only do so, but they are the only animals that can. They can do so because of a complex chain of bones that fasten the lower jaw to the skull and which may be moved out sideways. This increases the size of the mouth opening. Then, too, the throat is very elastic. Actually, in swallowing the snake draws itself forward over its prey instead of using its tongue to swallow, as we do. If you have never watched a snake feed, do so by all means. It is a worthwhile experience.

"Spread-head," "blow-snake," "puff adder," "hissing viper"—take your pick, for they are all names of what is probably the most notorious and most widely feared of American snakes. But what's in a name? The snake is completely harmless and cannot be induced to bite whatever the provocation. Then why is it so feared? Because it is a most capable actor, and when met for the first time, it demonstrates histrionic talents that would deceive anyone.

The names I mentioned above are some of the names given to a serpent usually known as the hog-nosed snake. It is stout of body, slow moving, and superficially viperlike in appearance, with an upturned shovel-like snout. It is generally found in dry, sandy settings, but it may, on occasion, get into your garden or back yard.

Unlike other snakes, which silently glide away when encountered, the hog-nosed does not seek to escape but holds its ground, flattening and spreading its head and the forepart of its body to twice its normal width, in the manner of a cobra. At the same time it inflates its lungs to capacity with air, which is then expelled with a loud hiss.

And should you approach it ever so closely, it will strike out at you but always with its mouth closed. It puts on a fearful display of ferocity and a most amazing performance, for it is sheer bluff. If you reach down as if to take hold of it, it may hit your hand, but it will not bite. This is not the extent of the snake's acting ability, however, for if further molested it opens its mouth wide, sticks out its tongue, contorts its body, writhing as though in agony, becoming covered with all sorts of dirt and debris, and rolls over on its back.

It now lies perfectly still as if dead. Pick it up, and it hangs limp and apparently lifeless in your hand and remains that way even though you handle it somewhat roughly. But roll it over on its belly or place it on the ground right side up, if you have picked it up, and it will immediately turn over on its back again. If you have completely ignored it and retreated a few steps, it will, if left undisturbed for a few minutes, raise its head and, seeing no danger, crawl away.

It is somewhat difficult to appraise the survival value of such behavior, for we know little of its effect on other animals. The effect on us seems to be another matter, since its apparent show of hostility has earned for it a widespread and unwarranted malignant reputation.

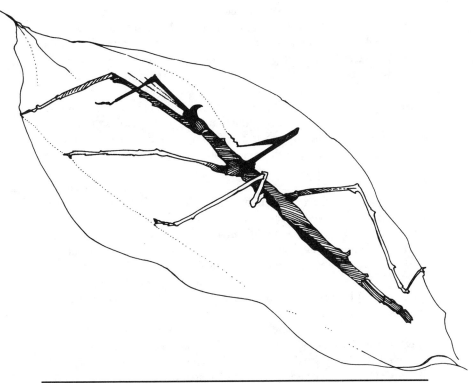

Walking Stick
The stick that walks

Few animals arouse our curiosity as much as the walking stick does when we come upon it—which we seldom do. Not that it is a rare insect. It just happens that it is one of the finest examples of protective resemblance that we have and so escapes detection unless we find one by chance.

From its very name we can conjure up in our mind's eye a stick with legs, and we will have a fair idea of what the insect looks like. When resting on a tree or bush, it looks so much like a twig that it takes an exceptionally good eye to detect it. Even the best of us usually pass it by without seeing it.

Walking sticks are primarily tropical and subtropical

insects. In the U.S. we have a species that measures when full grown about three inches or a little more in length with a body not much more than an eighth of an inch in width. This is a pygmy compared to some tropical species, especially the one found in the Malay Peninsula, which has been known to reach a length of thirteen inches.

Except for a species that occurs in Florida, the walking sticks found in the United States, and there are several, are wingless. The more exotic species have wings, and in many of these the wings resemble leaves. The antennae and legs of our common species are threadlike, and we may well wonder how it can walk on such spindly legs. Actually it doesn't do much walking and prefers to remain quietly at rest in one place.

When the young emerge from the eggs in spring they are a uniform pale yellowish green in color. As a rule they remain near the ground and drop readily when disturbed. They mature rather rapidly. As they get older, they change to a gray or brown to match the color of the leaves in autumn and the twigs on which they normally rest and which they resemble, the front legs being extended straight out to enhance the illusion. Sometimes the males, which are smaller than the females, remain green, and thus are not quite so well protected.

The walking stick lives on green leaves, but rarely is the insect sufficiently abundant to cause any serious injury. Considering how well protected it is, or seemingly so, in form and color, and that there is always an abundance of food available, we may well wonder why it is not more common. It is true that there have been instances where the insect has been found in large numbers, but such abundance has been localized.

In spite of its camouflaging shape and color, the walking stick is eaten by fifteen different species of birds as well as by lizards and rodents, so perhaps protective resemblance is not as effective as it is supposed to be. Whatever the answer, we never know where or when we will find it. Go out into your garden or backyard and you may find one if you look carefully, or you may not find one for days. But you never know when one will pop in. Should you find one at any time, handle it carefully, for the legs are fragile and break off easily. The insect can grow new ones, but they are never as strong as the original ones.

Woodchuck
The laziest of animals

I have yet to hear anyone say something complimentary about the woodchuck. Indeed, everyone I meet seems to think he is an unmitigated nuisance. And whenever I come to his defense, they bluntly query me as to whether I have ever tried to cultivate a vegetable garden in competition with his destructive activities.

     I will admit that the woodchuck frequently does considerable damage to various cultivated crops, especially vegetables in field and garden, and often proves annoying to the farmer by digging holes and earth mounds in the fields and by feeding on and trampling down grasses and grains. But after all, he commits these depredations without malice and simply because he has to live. Who can blame him, either, if we tempt him with delicacies, and he succumbs to temptation.

I would not want to see the woodchuck go the way of the dodo, for to my mind he is a rather likable animal, in spite of being fat, lazy, and stupid. I think we would miss him were he to vanish forever from the scene. However, I do not believe that is likely to happen, even though every farmer and gardener is against him, to say nothing of the hunters, who consider him fair game. He can more than hold his own, since his natural enemies, with the exception of the fox, have largely vanished from his domain.

It is unnecessary to describe the woodchuck, for he is a familiar inhabitant of fields and grassy hillsides; there are few who are not acquainted with him. Those who live in the country know him well, and what city dweller, while on a tramp through the fields in spring or summer, has not caught a glimpse of a woodchuck waddling away to his burrow or possibly to his den in some wall or stone heap, which he sometimes prefers for a summer home.

The woodchuck is a lazy animal and likes to spend the day taking his ease. He usually feeds in the morning, coming out soon after sunrise, while the dew is still on the ground, and again in the evening. The middle of the day he is likely to spend resting in his burrow or den, although he may come out while the sun is high in the sky to sun himself. He does not, as a rule, go far from his home, although in the spring, like many of us, he may get wanderlust and travel about. He has a great deal of curiosity and often sits upright on his hind feet to scan his surroundings, remaining in such a position for a long time, motionless as a statue.

Despite his sluggish and stupid nature, the woodchuck is not necessarily easy to capture. If attacked, he will seek his burrow with frantic haste, his black heels twinkling in the sunshine. If his avenue of escape is cut off and he is cornered, he is no mean adversary and will fight savagely, his strong, sharp incisors proving defensive weapons with which he can inflict severe wounds, as more than one dog has discovered to his sorrow.

The woodchuck is one of our most famous winter sleepers, and early in summer he begins eating enormous quantities of food so that he may acquire a thick layer of fat to see him through the period of hibernation. As the first frosts blacken tender plants, he becomes more and more sluggish and appears above the ground with decreasing frequency, until at last he retires to his burrow for good, usually not to reappear until spring.

Should the weather in February be mild, however, he may come out of his burrow but will return to it if cold weather sets in again. This appearance of the woodchuck in February has led to the popular belief that the animal comes out to make his weather observation—a legend that seems to have originated with the blacks of the eastern middle states—and that if he sees his shadow, we are in for six more weeks of winter. As a weather prognosticator, the woodchuck is most unreliable, but the legend nevertheless has found a widespread popularity and has earned for him a day on our calendar (Ground-hog Day, February 2), the only animal, incidentally, to be so honored.

Years ago the woodchuck usually had his home in the woods, where he fed on the tender bark and roots of various kinds. Today we are more likely to find him in the fields and meadows or in grassy hillsides, especially where bordering woodlands offer a safe retreat. Doubtless a change in address was motivated by a desire to be nearer the farmer's clover patch, where a living could be obtained with a minimum of effort. The garden, too, was close at hand and perhaps had something to do with it, for there he could occasionally taste the juicy peas, beans, and lettuce of which he is very fond and especially melons for which he has a special liking.

The woodchuck's home is a burrow or tunnel that may vary in length from ten to twenty-five feet, which he excavates under stone walls, rocks, ledges, or old stumps, sometimes even out in the grass-grown fields, and is usually dug two or three feet below the surface of the ground. He excavates with his front feet, which are armed with claws, and pushes the loose earth backward and out with his hind feet. The earth thus pushed out accumulates in a little telltale mound that advertises the location of his home. The burrow ends in a rounded chamber about a foot in diameter, large enough for several animals to turn around in comfortably. There are a number of branching galleries or tunnels, some also ending in rounded chambers lined with grass and leaves. Others lead to the surface of the ground and provide observation outlets or back doors through which the woodchuck can escape if his quarters are invaded by the fox, mink, or skunk. These back doors differ from the main entrance in that they are usually concealed and are not surrounded by telltale mounds of earth, as they are opened from below.

The young are born in the latter part of April or about the first of May. They are blind and helpless and weigh about an ounce when born, but in a month or so, they are sufficiently grown to leave the nest. Then on some bright sunny day, they are taken to the entrance of the burrow by their mother and with wondering brown eyes gaze for the first time on the outside world.

This coming-out party is doubtless quite an event for the chucklings. The fragrance of the fields and meadows whisper to their awakening instincts of clover and sweet grass, while the merry tune of the bobolink and the whistle of the meadowlark or perhaps the song of the wren in a nearby orchard, rising above the hum of countless insects, announce the presence of other creatures in this new and strange world. Of the farmer's dog and their arch enemy, the fox, they have as yet no inkling. Mother, of course, is acquainted with both and, before permitting her young to venture from the entrance to their burrow, scans the surroundings carefully. If satisfied that there is nothing to fear, she leads the way to the grass and begins to nibble the clover leaves.

The chucklings, instinctively imitating her, also take to nibbling the juicy leaves and eat as much as they can, stuffing their little stomachs to the bursting point. When they can eat no more, they are shepherded back to their burrow, not to enter, however, but to play about in the grass or to sun themselves, according to their mood, the mother meanwhile keeping them close to the entrance so that she can hustle them down into the burrow upon the approach of an enemy.

Thereafter they venture forth each day and, partly by imitating their mother and partly through instinct and experience, receive their education in how to get along in a world in which they soon must fend for themselves. They learn to distinguish the plants that are good for them, either as food or medicine, from those they should leave alone and also to recognize among the many sounds that come to their ears those that spell danger.

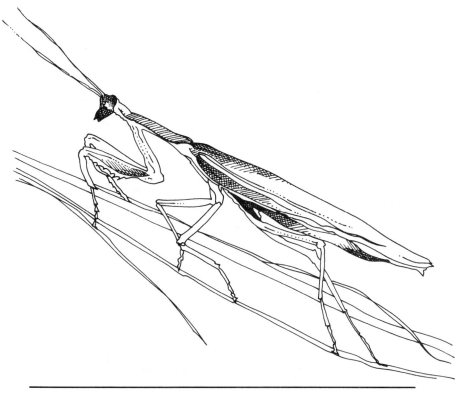

Praying Mantis
The deceiver

I have many animal visitors to my garden and back yard during the year, but none has been more regular over the years than the praying mantis. The name of this insect, for that is what it is, alludes to the devout attitude that it generally assumes when at rest. It is anything but pious, however, being one of the most highly predatory members of the insect world. Watch it sometime. You will observe that the moment an unsuspecting insect comes within reach, the front legs, which are ordinarily held in a posture that suggests prayer, are quickly extended forward in a sudden lunge to clasp the victim, which is then conveyed to the mantis's mouth. Perhaps the insect should be called preying mantis instead—it would be more appropriate.

That the praying mantis is well adapted for a predatory existence is obvious from just a casual glance at its front legs. They are exceptionally large and are capable of being stretched in various directions in a most amazing fashion. Moreover, they are armed with sharp, toothlike spines that clamp into a victim with a traplike finality. Once caught, there is little chance for a victim to escape.

The mantis is the only insect that can look back over its shoulders and see in practically any direction, so it does not really matter where its prey alights if within reaching distance of its formidable legs. The mantis, as a rule, does not pursue its prey, but waits patiently for it to come within reach. Sometimes, however, a prospective meal may alight just beyond reach. At such times the mantis goggles its large eyes at the prey, then begins a swaying motion, and with exaggerated care and slowness starts to crawl toward its victim a step at a time until it is near enough to extend its deadly forelegs.

We have our own American species of mantids, one being found in the South and several in the West. Those that occur in the East have come to us from China and Europe. The praying mantis feeds on insects of all kinds and, because it consumes many harmful ones, is generally considered to be a beneficial species. At times, however, it will at times also devour some useful insects, such as the honey bees and ladybird beetles. The mantid, as a matter of fact, is so carnivorous that the female will not hesitate to eat her mate after mating if he is not alert enough to escape her clutches.

The praying mantis overwinters in the egg stage. The eggs, some two hundred or more in number, are deposited in a mass or cluster and are overlaid with a hard covering of silk. The egg mass is shaped like a short, broad cornucopia of dried foam and is usually attached to twigs or stems of plants, although I have found them fastened to other objects, such as garden chairs.

If you have never watched a praying mantis feed, do so sometime—it is worth observing as a real lesson in predation.

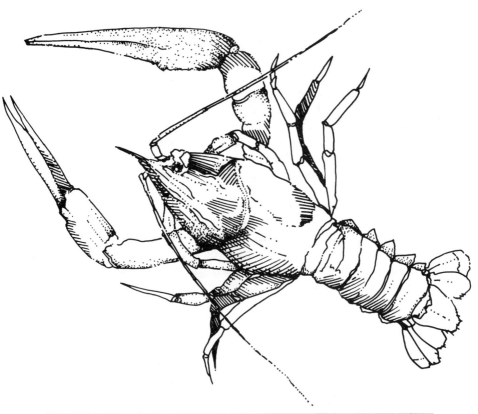

Crayfish
The replica

Although most of us have heard of the crayfish, because it is a common inhabitant of the ponds, lakes, streams, and swamps of North America, few of us have seen the living animal, for it usually lives under a flattish stone or in a shallow burrow in the gravelly bottom. From such a sheltered situation it lies in wait for a passing fish, a water insect, or some other aquatic animal, which it catches with a pair of pincerlike claws without at all exposing itself. Its food also consists of dead plant and animal matter, and hence it is useful as a scavenger.

The crayfish is essentially nocturnal in habit, although on cloudy days and in shady streams it may often be seen prowling about on the bottom by day. For the most part, however, it is a secretive animal, preferring to remain hidden and to lie in wait for some prospective prey. In turn it has many enemies, such as various fishes, wading birds, frogs, turtles, raccoons, otters, and mink. I suppose we should also include humans, although in our country it has not become as popular an article of food as it is in Europe. Incidentally, it is also known as the crawfish.

The crayfish is a relative of the lobster, crab, and shrimp, and with the exception of the southern freshwater prawns, it is the only freshwater representative of the group known as the *decapods*, so named because of their ten feet. Except for size and minor differences, the crayfish is so much like the lobster in structure and habits that it has often been referred to as the freshwater edition of the lobster. It is practically a replica of the lobster. Like the lobster its distinguishing feature is the first pair of legs, each of which is provided with a conspicuous and formidable nipper or pincer, which serve as both offensive and defensive weapons.

There are a number of species of crayfish. Some of them appear transluscent, and others are heavily pigmented with black, brown-red, orange-red, or blue, frequently with mottling. At times they may exhibit a great deal of color variation, one species ranging through all the colors mentioned above. Quite often the color or shade is determined by the nature of the animal's background, the result of the chromatophores' (the light-sensitive color cells) ability to open and close and thus expose varying amounts of the pigment granules that they contain.

Some crayfish live in lakes and some in both slow and swift streams; others prefer muddy ponds and ditches and burrow into the banks if the ponds and ditches dry up; and still others burrow in wet meadows and never go into the water. Those that occur in water are rarely found in water over five feet deep.

The burrows of crayfish vary in size and in complexity of structure, and range in depth from a few inches to eight to ten feet, depending on the water level. In any event, the terminal chamber in which the crayfish spends the day must be wet. The excavated soil is usually piled up around the entrance and sometimes forms what are called chimneys, which may be of considerable height. Some species of crayfish excavate burrows that extend below the frost line and down to the ground water. In winter, and in summer when lakes and streams recede, such crayfish enter their tunnels, plug up the openings, and retire to their underground cisterns of ground water, where they remain in a more or less inactive state. In winter the crayfish are sluggish and lethargic, move slowly about, and increase in size very little or not at all, and hence do not molt.

Some species of crayfish mate in the fall and spawn in the spring, while others mate throughout the year. It appears that the males are unable to distinguish the sexes during the breeding season—they try to mate with any crayfish that they encoutner. At the time of mating the sperms are transferred to the seminal receptacles (saclike organs that receive and store sperms) of the female, and when the eggs are laid several weeks or several months later, they are then fertilized. The eggs are not deposited in the water but are attached to the swimmerets (abdominal appendages that function as swimming organs) by means of a sticky substance and are aerated by being moved back and forth in the water. At this time, the crayfish, like the lobster, is said to be "in berry." The eggs hatch in two months or so, and the young crayfish, which have the form of their parents, attach themselves to the swimmerets and are carried about until they can shift for themselves.

Crayfish are able to form habits and to modify them, as has been shown by certain simple experiments. Apparently the chief factors in the formation of habits are to be the senses of smell, taste, touch, and sight. They learn by experience and modify their behavior quickly or slowly, according to how familiar they are with given conditions.

There are several species of cave crayfish in the United States that are of more than passing interest because of their striking modifications. These crayfish are all blind, their eyes being atrophied and their eyestalks more or less undeveloped. They are, moveover, all light colored, pigmentation being absent. Their claws are not too well developed, but their antennae are long and highly specialized (as might be expected) as tactile organs. Generally, they are small species.

Hawks
Victims of persecution

I can think of few sights more magnificent than that of a hawk soaring high in the sky. Sailing on outstretched wings in wide circles, the bird is a picture of repose in motion and a never-failing source of delight. I have often paused to watch the flight of a hawk following it as it sailed around, ascending and descending, balancing in the cool currents high above the earth, sometimes stationary on motionless wings and sometimes climbing an invisible spiral staircase until it was a mere speck in the sky. Then suddenly it would lift its wings above its back and plummet toward the earth with meteoric speed as it caught sight of a prospective meal.

   It is almost uncanny how the hawk floating high in the sky

can see a meadow mouse in a field far below. It has unusually keen eyesight and can see a moving object at a considerable distance. What is more, as fast as a mouse may be, the hawk is even faster, and can drop upon it like a thunderbolt out of a clear sky.

Up until quite recently the hawks were regarded as destructive pests to be destroyed at every opportunity. Poultry raisers believed that they fed almost exclusively upon barnyard birds, and hunters labored under the misconception that all hawks preyed upon game birds and therefore should be shown no mercy. We have come a long way since then but apparently not far enough. Some of us recognize the hawks as friends and allies in our warfare against the various pests of farm and garden, but there are still far too many who look upon these birds as a nuisance.

There are certain species of hawks, it is true, that will occasionally kill a game bird, but the harm they do in this direction is more than offset by the good they do in removing game birds that are suffering from contagious diseases. It is also true that some of the hawks will occasionally raid a poultry yard, but again, the harm they do in this respect is more than balanced by the vast number of rodents and harmful insects they consume. Thus, for instance, a report of the United States Department of Agriculture showed that of 220 stomachs of the red-shouldered hawk that were examined, only 3 contained the remains of poultry; 102 contained mice; 92 contained insects; 40 had moles and other small mammals; 39 batrachians; 20 reptiles; 16 spiders; 12 birds; 7 crayfish; 3 fish; 2 offal; 1 earthworms; and 14 were empty. Much the same can be said of the red-tailed hawk, 60 percent of whose food consists of injurious mammals, such as mice and gophers, and only 7 percent of poultry, which are usually old and disabled.

Both the red-shouldered and the red-tailed hawks are large birds, the former recognized by its cinnamon-brown epaulets, a blackish tail crossed by five or six narrow white bars, and barred wing feathers; the latter by its dark brown wings and a brilliant cinnamon-colored tail with a black bar across it near the end, and its silvery white underside. Both birds spend a great deal of time perching on dead branches from which they can watch for mice as they creep through the meadows, chipmunks as they run along stone walls, or young rabbits as they play about the edges of woods. They are also fond of frogs and snakes and often sit on a branch overhanging a sluggish stream.

The hawks are eminently fitted for their predatory existence, having strong feet and sharp, curved talons with which to capture their prey and a very sharp, hooked beak for tearing apart the flesh. They are fearless and courageous birds and will not hesitate to contend with either human or animal if attacked. At such times they throw themselves over on their backs and with eyes gleaming savagely strike at their enemy with vicious thrusts of their bill and talons. They are capable of inflicting severe wounds.

From our viewpoint, the broad-winged hawk is even more blameless than either the red-shouldered or the red-tailed for of sixty-five stomachs examined, no game birds or poultry appeared at all, and small birds were found in only two. The rough-legged hawk, the marsh hawk, the osprey, or fish hawk, the sparrow hawk, or American kestrel, and Swainson's hawk are also without taint.

The American kestrel, or sparrow hawk, is one of the smallest of our hawks and also one of the most unsuspicious, in this latter respect being much like the robin. I have frequently come upon the hawk perched on a dead branch or fence post, occasionally jerking its tail as it scanned the field before it for some luckless grasshopper or meadow mouse. I recall one time when I watched one from the cover of a thicket. Suddenly, without warning, it launched itself into the air, hovered for a minute, and then dropped like a stone toward the ground where it became lost from view in the grass. But in a twinkling it reappeared with a mouse struggling in its talons and flew back to its perch to feast in leisure.

If dissatisfied with its hunting, the kestrel will take off over the fields in a graceful, swift flight, shrilly calling "killy-killy-killy-killy." Now and then it will pause, suspended in midair like a kingfisher, scanning the ground before continuing past the thickets at the edge of the woods or through the distant orchard to become lost from sight.

White-foot Mouse
A friendly visitor

We dislike having mice in our home, for we regard them as unwelcome, somewhat loathsome creatures, and we are inclined to view all mice in much the same light. But wrongly so, for the white-foot of our woodlands is far from repulsive. On the contrary, he is a most appealing little animal.

       Dressed in a spotless robe of grayish fawn set off by the pure white of his underparts, and with a natural grace and agility of movement that is in keeping with his trim form, and a keen expression in his large black eyes, he is undoubtedly the most attractive and interesting of our native mice. Moreover, he has a gentle disposition and is one of the most unsuspicious of living creatures, as you will find if he visits your garden or back yard and you become acquainted with him. Should you make friendly overtures to him, he will soon become quite tame and confiding and will like nothing better than to climb about your person and hide in your pockets. All in all, I doubt if anyone can find a more delightful little animal of the wild unless it is the saucy, impish chipmunk.

If you are not acquainted with the white-foot, also known as the deermouse, you will readily recognize him by his contrasting upper and lower parts and his white feet. Do not expect to see him during the daytime, for he is essentially nocturnal in habits, although occasionally he is about on cloudy days. And do not expect to see him in the fields and meadows either. His home is in the woods, although he often frequents shrubby pastures if they are fringed by dense hedgerows. Hence we must live in a rural or semirural area not too far from his natural habitat if we expect him to pay us a visit. Evergreens and hardwoods, thickets of blueberry bushes, and dense hedgerows are his favorite spots, and for this reason, he is also called the wood mouse.

The home of the white-foot is often in a half-rotted stump, among hollow roots, or in the cavity of a venerable beech. He may also, particularly in winter, appropriate an abandoned bird's nest, which he deftly caps over with leaves or thistledown and thus provides himself with a snug retreat in which to sleep away the day. He may, at times, not even wait for winter to take possession of some nest but will do so in summer. In fact, he won't necessarily even wait for the rightful owners to leave but will drive them out by eating the eggs or the young birds, for the white-foot is omnivorous in his eating habits.

He may also make use of a squirrel's deserted nest, high among the oak boughs. Sometimes he will even build his own nest in a thick tangle of bushes anywhere from four to ten feet above the ground, a favorite location being a gently inclined vine, such as wild grape, which affords a natural and easy highway to his home. He begins his nest with a platform of loose twigs laid crosswise for a foundation, although sometimes he makes use of an old bird's nest, very often that of the catbird, for a foundation. When finished, his nest is slightly globular in shape and is composed of dried leaves, grasses, moss, and fibrous barks of various kinds compactly put together and most attractive.

The white-foot has a varied diet though his chief food appears to be the nutlets, berries, and seeds that are abundant in any woods in summer; during this time of the year he also consumes vast quantities of insects. As fall approaches, he begins to store up vast quantities of all sorts of edibles, for he is active all winter and must have an ample supply to see him through. However, though his retreat may be stored with nuts and seeds, he still forages for food when the snow is on the ground. On the bitterest nights of winter, when countless stars form a canopy over the tree tops and biting winds howl through the stiff branches that creak and groan, and with snow piled high over the tangled brush, he is abroad, skipping along the snow from tree to tree. Only during stormy weather will he remain in his snug retreat.

Ladybird Beetles
The dedicated

I seldom hear anyone mention the ladybirds any more, and I have more or less come to the conclusion that people today are not too well acquainted with these colorful and useful insects. When I was a boy, it seemed that everyone knew them. I can recall my mother saying that they brought luck and money whenever they appeared in the house, as they frequently did. I don't imagine she had too much faith in the belief but merely repeated a superstition that goes back to the Middle Ages when the beetles were dedicated to the Virgin and became known as the "beetles of the blessed lady." Anyway, it was one of the first, if not the first, insect I came to know, and whenever any of us children saw one of them we would invariably exclaim;

Ladybird, ladybird!
Fly away home.
Your house is on fire.
Your children do roam.

This couplet appears to have had its origin in the practice of the hop growers of the Old Country who burned the vines after the hops had been harvested so as to clear the fields for the next planting. By doing so they also got rid of the aphids or plant lice that infested the vines as well as the young (children) of the ladybirds that prey on them. Which leads us to add to the above couplet:

Except little Nan,
Who sits in a pan
Weaving gold laces
As fast as she can.

Nan being the yellow pupa who cannot roam, as she is fastened to the plant by the handle of the "pan." The ladybird, of course, has no home and never did have one, but her "children" do roam, in search of plant lice and scale insects on which to feed.

The ladybirds are also called ladybird beetles and ladybugs, the last name being something of a misnomer, because they are not, technically speaking, bugs. The term *bugs* is applied by entomologists to a group of insects quite unlike the beetles. Ladybirds are so common and abundant that they hardly need to be described. They are for the most part rather small insects, round or oval, or hemispherical in shape. Their color is generally red or yellow with contrasting black spots on their wing covers, or else black with white, red, or yellow spots, though some species are quite variable. Their bright colors are presumed to be warning signs to birds, for birds drop them immediately upon picking them up, apparently finding the strong-smelling liquid that the ladybirds give off quite distasteful. Hold a ladybird in your hand for a few moments or squeeze it ever so slightly, and it will exude a liquid from the leg joints and other parts of its body that will stain your skin yellow.

It has been said that in a very general way and subject to many exceptions the ladybirds that are red or yellow with black spots feed on plant lice or aphids, and those that are wholly black or black with red or yellow spots feed on scale insects.

As is the case with many insects, the young, or larvae, are quite unlike the fully grown insects in appearance. They are small in size, fairly long, shaped something like an alligator, rather velvety to look at, and covered with warts and spines. They have six short, queer legs that seem more suited for clasping a twig than for walking—all of which you can see for yourself by looking at them with a hand lens. They are usually black in color and prettily marked with blue, orange, or yellow.

As a rule, the female ladybirds will lay their eggs near a colony of aphids so that when they hatch the young will have a ready access to food. When the eggs do hatch, the young ladybirds usually descend on the helpless aphids like a pack of hungry wolves. Occasionally the aphids may move elsewhere before the eggs hatch. Then the larvae have to go in search of them, which they do most energetically for the simple reason that they are famished.

Both the young and adult ladybirds are predaceous to a high degree and are numbered among our most beneficial insects because of the large numbers of aphids and scale insects they consume. Various records have been kept recording the number of aphids a larva can eat in a day, and it appears that on the average a single larva can do away with from twenty to fifty aphids during this time; an adult twice as many. Moreover, ladybirds also eat the eggs of the aphids, and one adult can devour as many as one hundred daily. Since a female ladybird can have from one hundred to two hundred young ones, a colony of these insects can be a real asset to any gardener who is faced with the problem of getting rid of aphids.

Just how valuable the ladybirds can be was demonstrated by a classic example of some years ago. Toward the close of the last century the citrus growers of California were suddenly threatened with the loss of their crops by the ravages of the cottony cushion scale, which somehow had managed to get into our country from abroad. Our native species of ladybirds were not interested in the pest, various insecticidal sprays proved ineffective, and other methods were equally unsuccessful. So the problem became one of finding some insect that would prey on the pest and thus keep it under control. After considerable searching, such an insect was finally discovered in the form of an Australian ladybird generally known as the vedalia beetle. It was brought to California, though not without some trouble, and did its job so well that soon it almost died out for lack of food; as a matter of fact, it became necessary for the state of California to undertake the artificial propagation of the ladybird to insure a continuous supply. Millions of these beetles are now reared and liberated each year in various orchards in an effort to keep the cottony scale insect under control. The introduction of the vedalia beetle to prey on the scale insect was the first example of what is now known as biological control, that is, the control of an insect pest by means of another insect instead of by insecticides or by crop rotation.

Opossum
The living fossil

Sometimes an animal's behavior leads to an expression that becomes part of our language, such as the phrase "playing possum." As most of us know, the opossum often feigns death when threatened or molested by an enemy.

It is a strange and striking performance. The animal lies down, opens his mouth, draws back his lips from glittering white teeth, allows his tongue to loll out, and tightly closes his eyes. To all appearances he seems quite lifeless. With his black, withered ears, skinny tail, and the faded colorless look of his fur, anyone might easily believe that he has been dead for a long time. Even if picked up and dropped from a short height, he falls to the ground in a limp heap.

That the ruse is effective against predatory animals that react only to live and moving prey and find the apparently lifeless opossum unattractive as food cannot be denied, but no protective device or form of behavior is 100 percent perfect. Doubtless the opossum escapes many an enemy by practicing this form of deceit, but he is also easy prey for his many enemies, including humans and their dogs; indeed, it is rather surprising that the animal has not become extinct.

We think of the opossum as an animal of the Deep South, and rightly so, for he is common and abundant throughout the southern states. But in recent years, the opossum has been extending his range northward and can now be found throughout most of the eastern half of the United States, though probably only sporadically.

He may be more abundant there than we realize, for the animal is shy and secretive. The first intimation we may have of his presence in our locality is to find him in the beam of our auto headlights or to see a dead one on the highway. He is essentially an animal of the open woods, swamps, and waste lands, but being an adaptable creature, does very well in farming country if there is sufficient cover for shelter and for hunting food. Sometimes he invades a village or town and then frequently pays a visit to our garden and back yard in search of something to eat.

But even in settled country, the opossum is not often seen, as he sleeps all day and only bestirs himself at night when the need for food arises. He shows little discrimination when it comes to food—he will eat anything. His life appears to be one gastronomic delight after another, and perhaps it is well that it is so. The animal has many enemies, and were he limited in his choice of food, survival could well hang in the balance.

Climbing is second nature to the animal, and he hunts as well up in the trees as on the ground. What makes him an adept climber is the opposable toe on the hind feet and his prehensile tail. The opossum's home may be a hollow tree or log, or a cavity in the ground or even under a building. The young at birth are like tiny sightless embryos; they climb into their mother's pouch and attach themselves to her nipples. When about two months old, they have acquired a fine hair coat, and their eyes open, but they still remain attached to the nipples for two months or more, when they begin to move about freely and to eat solid food. They suckle for another mouth, however, before leaving their mother to take up a separate existence. During this time they often travel with her, clinging to her fur, occasionally with their tails wrapped around hers as she holds it forward over her back.

Actually the opossum has no business being in North America. A pouched animal, or marsupial, it is the only one on the continent; with one or two exceptions all other marsupials are found in Australia, where they seem to live a more or less uninhibited life. Perhaps that is where the opossum rightly belongs. But at some time in the dim and remote past the opossum found himself in North America and has remained ever since. One of the least intelligent of our wild animals, how he has ever managed to survive in the midst of numerous enemies and in spite of climatic tumults and geologic upheavals is something of a mystery. Except for his larger size, he is almost the same as his ancestor of millions of years ago; he is rightly a "living fossil."

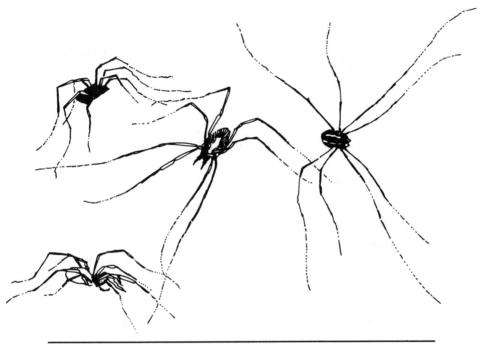

Harvestman
The daddy with the long legs

I don't know how, when, or where the animal got its name, but I knew it when a boy as the daddy with the long legs or, more precisely, as daddy longlegs. The name harvestman, or harvestmen (when we speak of more than one), would appear to be preferable and has been given to it because it is seen in greater numbers during the harvesting time of the year. The French know the harvestmen as the haymakers; the Germans, as the pseudospiders (because of their resemblance to spiders); and the English, as harvest spiders and shepherd spiders.

      The young, which emerge in the spring from overwintering eggs, are very timid creatures and usually hide under stones and other objects until they become full grown in late summer. Then they become more venturesome and come out into the open. And as I have just said, it is because they are more noticeable at this time of the year—harvest time—that they are known by the more acceptable name of harvestmen; in Europe a good harvest is believed to follow their appearance in large numbers, and it is considered unlucky to kill one. At any rate, we see them now running over boulders in the pasture—their favorite hunting grounds—in fields and along woodland borders, indeed everywhere, even in our gardens and back yards, where they may be observed climbing up an old apple tree, or clambering over a wood-pile or rubbish heap.

The harvestmen resemble spiders, with which they are often confused. They may be readily recognized by their long stiltlike legs and the fact that, unlike the spiders and other insects, their three body regions, namely head, thorax, and abdomen, are all fused into a single unit that looks much like a grain of wheat.

Watching these animals run over the ground, it doesn't seem possible that they can support their bodies on those eight long, thin, fragile-appearing legs and that they can move over the ground with such speed. One would expect them to get their legs caught in the grass blades, and now and then they do. But this is a trifling matter, for if the harvestman cannot extricate itself, it will merely "throw off" a leg and grow a new one.

The legs, of course, are much stronger than we would suspect and, strangely enough, separate quite easily from the body. That, combined with their unusual length, has led some observers to believe they serve as a sort of protective fence when the animal is attacked: The enemy grasps a leg as the nearest thing to seize and is left with it as the harvestman "throws it off" and escapes.

In spite of its stiltlike legs, the harvestman does not carry its body very high above the ground when it walks but instead carries it low down, with the middle part of the legs high in the air. If disturbed, it will then stand on six legs and wave the second pair about in the air, which would suggest that the tips of these legs are provided with organs that are sensitive to touch.

Unlike the spiders, the harvestmen do not have any silk glands and hence cannot spin webs or retreats. They feed, for the most part, on dead insects but are also known to kill small ones for food and to suck juices from various soft fruits and vegetables.

Before the first frost, the females lay their eggs in the ground, under stones, and in the crevices of wood. Unlike the eggs of the spiders, they do not hatch until the following spring. In the North the winter cold kills the adults, with one exception: There is one northern species that lives through the winter as an adult. In the South, most harvestmen hibernate in some safe retreat, for instance, beneath rubbish.

Mud Wasps
The masons

According to the dictionary, a dauber is one who daubs, the word *daub* meaning to cover, coat, or smear with a soft, adhesive substance, such as plaster or mud, in a somewhat rough, unskillful manner. Hence the term *mud dauber* would appear to be an uncomplimentary one when applied to an insect that makes use of mud with which to fashion its nest. Yet in spite of its rather slovenly external appearance, the nest is cleverly and skillfully constructed. In a word, the mud dauber, as we know it, is a real artisan.

      The mud dauber is a thread-waisted wasp, black or brown in color, with yellow spots and legs. It first puts in an appearance in late spring or early summer, depending on the locality. I often see it flitting about the flowers in my garden or sunning itself on the railing of the porch or on a fence. It has the curious habit of jerking its wings constantly as it walks. Perhaps that is to display the beautiful black wings, which shimmer in the sunlight with a rainbowlike iridescence. Perhaps it is just plain nervousness, for this wasp also has the curious habit of turning around constantly as if expecting to be attacked from the rear.

As the days go by, I begin to listen for the female wasp's singing whenever I go into my garage, and if I hear her, I know she is hard at work. She does not actually sing, of course, in the sense that she produces sound by means of a vocal apparatus. She produces a sound by vibrating her wings, and this may be either high- or low-pitched, according to what she is doing. While fashioning her nest, she produces a high-pitched rasping, but when gathering mud with which to build it, she produces a faint hum, as if this is a task more to her liking.

The wasp builds her nest of mud collected from some nearby puddle. She gathers the mud with her jaws and mixes it with saliva, which seems to serve as a binder. She is also particular as to what kind of mud she uses—I have seen these wasps spend considerable time around a puddle, running up and down and digging here and there until they have found mud to their liking. When the wasp finds suitable mud, she rams her head down and with her jaws cuts out pellets about the size of sweet pea seeds. Anyone chancing upon a group of these wasps for the first time and seeing them standing on their heads and waving their tails in the air might well wonder what sort of rite they are performing.

Usually when I find my mud dauber at work, she has the foundation already in place. This has meant a large number of trips, for the amount of mud she can carry in her jaws at one time is limited. She works with her head and jaws, flattening the mud into a sort of pie until she feels satisfied that she has constructed a foundation upon which the cells may be safely built. In this particular case the foundation was attached to the wall of the garage, but the site of a nest may be on the side of a building, the rafter of a barn, or the wall or beam of an unfinished attic.

With the foundation finally completed, the mud dauber returns to the puddle for another load of mud and proceeds with great care and much squeaking to apply it on the foundation in the form of a ring. Returning to the puddle for more and more mortar, she fashions the pellets into a series of overlapping concentric rings until she has

constructed a neat earthen cell or tube, smooth inside but rough outside, some eighteen millimeters long and eleven wide, with a circular
entrance at one end six millimeters in diameter.

The wasp now lets the cell dry before she goes in search of a
spider with which to provision it. I have seen the daubers hunt diligently for spiders among the grasses and flowers and have often marvelled at the uncanny instinct that leads them to sting their unfortunate
victims so that they are paralyzed and yet remain alive. Having found a
spider, the wasp returns with it and thrusts it snugly into the far end of
the earthen tube, which is to be the spider's sarcophagus, and then
deposits on the soft abdomen a tiny, elongated, glistening yellow egg.
She flies away in search of another spider and, having found one,
returns with it and thrusts it into the tube on top of the first spider. She
repeats this performance until she has packed the tube full of spiders
after which she carefully seals it with mud. When she has completed
this task, she proceeds to fashion another tube and still another until the
nest contains several cells, all of which she provisions with spiders and
in each of which she lays an egg.

The eggs hatch within three days into tiny yellowish grubs,
which immediately begin to feed on the spiders. When there are no
more spiders left on which to gorge themselves, the grubs spin their
cocoons and eventually transform into adult mud daubers, chew their
way out of the cells, and fly away to start another generation of mud
daubers.

We have another thread-waisted wasp, a beautiful steel blue
species, that at one time was believed to build nests of mud until it was
discovered that instead, the female appropriates nests made by the mud
dauber. This blue wasp breaks into the mud dauber's cells, tossing out
the spiders that the dauber has so laboriously collected and then re-
stocks the cells with spiders that she, herself, collects. Hence we know
her as the blue burglar.

But there is a third species that does build her nest of mud.
She is a shiny black insect known as the pipe organ wasp. Like the mud
dauber, she constructs her cells in the form of tubes, but unlike the
mud dauber, she partitions them into sections each of which she stocks
with spiders and seals off, one at a time. At times her nest will consist
of but a single tube, but at other times the tubes will be constructed in
groups placed side by side. Frequently additional tubes are built on top
of them, and the entire nest then resembles a pipe organ.

The most advanced example of wasp masonry is the nest of
the jug builder, or potter wasp. It resembles a jug and is an exquisite

little object even to the naked eye but more so when viewed with a magnifying glass or hand lens. It is usually saddled on a twig—sometimes there may be a little row of them and frequently they may be attached to the sides of trees—and is about half an inch in diameter. It has a delicate liplike margin around the small opening and is worthy of the skill of a master craftsman, or perhaps I should say craftswoman. Although the inside walls are smooth, the outside ones have scattered tubercles possibly put there for the purpose of camouflage.

There are a number of species of potter wasps, but all are of moderate size with yellow, orange, or black markings. Once the nest has been completed, the wasp inserts her abdomen into the open neck of the jug and deposits an egg, which is suspended on a slender thread so that it hangs down in the cell in the manner of a ceiling droplight. The reason for suspending the egg in this manner is probably to prevent it from being injured by the caterpillars with which the wasp stocks the cell; though the caterpillars are paralyzed, they are not completely without movement. And like the mud dauber, when the wasp has completely filled the cell with caterpillars, which for the most part are small and usually not much more than a quarter of an inch long, she seals the cell with mud, leaving the egg to hatch and the emerging grub to feed and grow and eventually develop into an adult wasp, which escapes from the cell by eating a hole in the seal.

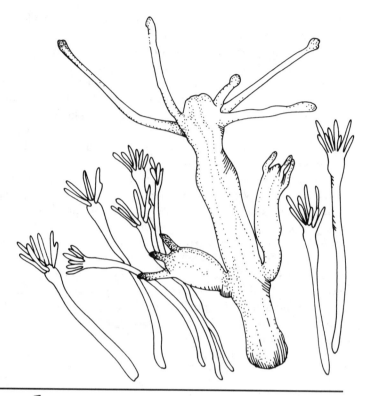

Hydra
The many-headed monster

Few of us realize what a vast assemblage of animals, and plants, inhabit an ordinary pond. As we stand by the water's edge we may see a few ducks in the distance and closer at hand a fish or two and perhaps a bullfrog. We are also sure to see the whirligigs and water striders, the diving beetles and backswimmers and water boatmen, maybe a water measurer and a caddis worm, even a diving spider. But there are countless others that we cannot see too well—animals that swim too fast or too near the bottom or that lurk among the submerged vegetation or crawl on logs and stones. Some are so small that we need a microscope to know that they are there at all; others appear as little specks; and still others look like tiny threads.

   Such minuscule threads are not threads at all but living

animals, which we know as the hydras. They are said to be named after the fabled monster slain by Hercules. If you know your Greek mythology, you will recall that the monster had nine heads, and if any one of them (except the middle one) was cut off, it grew two in its place. Our freshwater hydra has somewhat the same ability, for if the head end is split in two and the parts separated slightly, we have a "two-headed" hydra. I don't know how many heads the hydra can grow; theoretically there is no limit, but I imagine there must be one.

The hydra is a common inhabitant of ponds, slow streams, and still pools. If we look for it, we will usually find it attached to some water plant such as *nitella* or *elodea* or to the underside of a water lily. It looks like a small piece of thread about three-quarters of an inch long and frayed at one end.

Actually the hydra is a soft, transparent, cylindrical animal that can stretch itself to almost an inch in length and conversely contract until it is as small as a pinhead. It resembles an elastic tube. The frayed ends are a circlet of tentacles, which usually number six or seven, though in some species there may be as many as ten. In some hydras the tentacles are unusually extensible and can be stretched out from small blunt projections into very thin threads several times as long as the body. They act independently of each other and function in obtaining food. They convey the food to the mouth, which they surround, the mouth being a small circular pore in the center of a conical elevation (the hypostome). Both the mouth and the hypostome can be dilated to a fairly large diameter when the animal is in the act of swallowing its prey.

The opposite end of the hydra is known as the foot, or basal disc, and is usually attached to some object. It secretes a sticky substance that enables the animal to anchor itself to submerged plant stems, twigs, or leaves and even to the lower surface of the surface film of water. It also serves as a sort of locomotor organ: By clinging to an object with its sticky foot, the hydra can glide along the surface of the object and thus get from one place to another. It moves so slowly, however, that it is difficult to realize that it moves at all. In addition to the sticky substance, the foot also secretes a gas bubble enclosed by a film of mucus that lifts the hydra to the surface of the water, where it spreads out like a raft and hangs from the underside. In the foot is a pore, which is completely closed while the hydra remains attached to some object but opened when the animal suddenly releases its hold. It is likely that the function of this pore is to enable the animal to "blast" itself loose from its point of attachment.

The tentacles, which wave about almost continuously in

search of prey, are furnished with stinging cells, which occur on all parts of the hydra except the basal disc. When activated, they discharge a threadlike structure that either penetrates or entangles a prospective prey and thus helps in its capture.

Hydras are carnivorous animals and feed principally on small forms that live in the water, such as crustaceans, minute worms, small clams, and immature insects. Large hydras even capture and swallow small tadpoles and young fish. In 1740, Abbe Abraham Trembly, the pioneer student of hydras, described their capture of baby fishes. Today hydras sometimes appear by the thousands in hatchery troughs and create a great deal of havoc among the small fry.

After being swallowed, the prey passes into a capacious cavity, or stomach, where it is digested. The undigested parts are ejected through the mouth, as there is no special organ for this purpose. Hydras have an insatiable appetite and will eat so much that their bodies become distended, and they look like meal sacks, as one writer has put it. However, they will not always eat, even though food is available: It seems that they will eat only after a certain length of time has passed since their last meal. In other words, their reaction to the food stimulus is determined by their physiological condition.

Hydras react to stimuli, such as touch, light, and heat, in varying degree. They react positively to touch, contracting to the size of a pinhead but expanding once the stimulus has been removed. They also respond positively to bright light but will react negatively if the light is too strong. Such a reaction is of considerable importance, as evidenced by the fact that animals that serve as food are attracted to well-lighted areas. High temperatures produce a negative reaction, but it has been found that hydras will feed freely at low temperatures. Hydras taken from ice-covered lakes have been found to contain small insect larvae. They will also react positively to a weak electric current but, somewhat surprisingly, they show no response to water currents.

Hydras reproduce asexually by budding and sexually by the formation of germ cells (sperms and eggs). Both methods may occur at the same time in an individual hydra, but usually they occur at different seasons. In budding, the bud first appears as a slight bulge on the outside of the hydra. Once formed, it pushes out rapidly as a projection and soon develops a circlet of tentacles about its outer end. Even after the young hydra has acquired a mouth of its own and has begun feeding, it will remain attached to its parent for some time. When it is full grown, it will become detached and take up a separate existence.

In some species of hydras both sperms and eggs may be produced in the same individual, in other species in separate individuals. The sperms are formed in small conical or rounded elevations on the hydra called testes of which there may be as many as twenty or thirty, and in most species definite nipples develop through which the sperms escape. The eggs are produced in the ovary, a larger swelling near the foot, and only one egg is formed during a reproduction cycle. When the sperms are mature, they leave the testes and swim about in search of an egg; although several sperms may penetrate the egg membrane, only one enters the egg itself. Fertilization of the egg usually takes place soon after the egg is formed and while it is still attached to the parent. The early development of the young hydra begins under a sort of parental protection, but eventually the developing hydra, or embryo, becomes detached from the parent and falls to the bottom, where further development takes place and a young hydra is formed complete with tentacles and a mouth.

Hydras are obviously too small to be observed or studied in their natural habitat, but they may be observed at close range at home; all one has to do is to fill a bottle or jar with some pond water and transfer to it a spray or two of some water plant that has one or more of the animals attached to it. Hydras are fascinating animals to study and well worth a few moments of anyone's time.

Red Squirrel
The chatterer

It is much easier to buy mushrooms at the neighborhood store, but there have been times when I have preferred to go out into the woods and collect my own. Of course, to collect and eat such mushrooms you have to know which ones are safe to eat and which must be left alone. The red squirrel does not have such complications, for one mushroom is much like another to him, or so it seems. Although it appears that he favors the substantial *boleti*, he is not too discriminating, for he will eat other kinds, even the deadly—to us—*amanita*.

   It was on one of my mushroom-collecting trips that I happened to venture into the area occupied by one of these animals. At once he began to bark, spit, sputter, and growl at me from among the branches, at the same time observing my every move with a suspicious eye. And as I moved a little closer to him to get a better view, he flew into a rage. With convulsive movements, he stamped his feet and bounced about, scolding me with all the fury he could muster, giving voice to sounds which, if I could understand squirrel language, would probably have burned my ears.

The red squirrel is something of a paradox. On the one hand, he is a murderer, a thief, a nosey parker, unsociable (except during the mating season), jealous (he will ferociously guard and defend his domain and food caches), noisy, quarrelsome, mischievous, and insolent. On the other hand, he is industrious, persevering, thrifty, practical, ingenious, and intelligent and has a keen sense of humor and never-failing good spirits, his jollity seemingly undiminished by the fierce cold of a northern winter or the blistering heat of summer. He is, to be sure, an enigma and yet, with all his faults, a personable little animal.

The red squirrel is most at home in the evergreen forests, but he is an adaptable little animal and will occupy any area, such as various types of woodlands, as long as there is food and shelter. Should he visit our garden or back yard, it would be in keeping with his character. His home range is limited to some five hundred to seven hundred feet, and he rarely ventures farther except perhaps at mating time. As he is adapted in a number of ways for an arboreal existence, he spends most of his time in the trees, running up and down the trunks and along the branches, showing a surprising speed and endurance. At times he will jump from one tree to another with leaps of six to eight feet.

The red squirrel is an exceptionally good house builder. His favorite site is a natural tree cavity or one excavated by a woodpecker, in which he fashions a nest of grass and bark. Failing to find a suitable cavity, he will construct a roundish nest of leaves, pine needles, shreds of cedar or other bark, moss, dry grasses, and twigs in a whorl of many branches or in a witches-broom. He usually builds thirty or more feet above the ground but sometimes as low as six or eight feet. The nest is ingeniously contrived and, moreover, wind- and rain-proof.

In addition to a tree home, the red squirrel also excavates an underground burrow or den with many small rooms and passageways. Usually it is beneath a tree stump that can provide him with a strong roof. Why an animal with as much curiosity as the red squirrel should spend as much time underground as he does is a question.

The red squirrel is active by day and on moonlit nights.

With all his dashing about and noisy chatter, we may well wonder how he escapes his many enemies: weasel, mink, lynx, bobcat, marten, to say nothing of the house cat, the raptorial hawk, and even the big owl. Hunters with their rifles and youngsters with their slingshots are also numbered among his enemies.

The dietary of the red squirrel is a varied one that includes succulent growing twigs and buds, flower parts, seeds from trees and shrubs, insects of various kinds such as the pupae of moths, hornets, wasps, and bees, the larvae of wood boring beetles, plant lice, and occasionally grasshoppers, to say nothing of young birds and eggs. He also feeds on strawberries, different kinds of roots, the seeds of grasses, and a great variety of fungi. And in spring he is very fond of the sap of such trees as the maples and black birch, lapping it from a natural break in the bark or making a saucerlike incision in the bark on the upper side of a branch or stripping away the bark to make the sap flow.

The red squirrel is as industrious as the gray squirrel, and when the cool days of October warn of the approach of winter, he begins to prepare his winter home and to stock his larder so he will not go hungry. For though he is up and about even during the coldest days, there might be times when a driving storm will keep him home. Thus during the bright, sunny, cool days of autumn, we can see him collecting nuts or cutting and burying green pine cones in the damp earth, which prevents them from ripening. If they were allowed to ripen, the seeds would be scattered by the wind and lost. We can also see him collecting various fungi and deftly placing them in trees, where they will dry and be available for winter use.

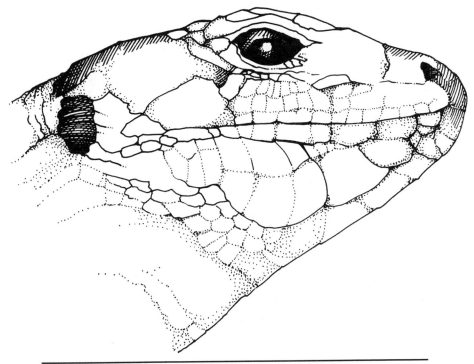

Lizards
The scamperers

We have all heard of the chameleon, but few of us have ever seen the living animal, nor are we likely to do so unless we visit Africa, Madagascar, or India, where the animal is to be found. Of course, we might see one in a zoo if the zoo has a fairly respectable reptile collection.

We have in many of the southern states what is erroneously called a chameleon. It is not a chameleon at all and is not even remotely related to the true chameleon of Africa; the only feature the two have in common is that they are both lizards. And yet this American animal is persistently called a chameleon because of its conspicuous and characteristic habit of undergoing rapid color changes so typical of the true chameleon. More accurately, it is an anole and should properly be known as the Carolina anole.

It is abundant in the South, occurring throughout what is known as the coastal plane, and may often be seen on fences, trees, shrubs, and vines as well as on the ground. It is a frequent visitor to our gardens and back yards, sometimes even entering our houses. There is a widespread and popular but erroneous belief that its color changes are influenced by the color of the animal's background or by the color of the object on which it may be resting. But that is not so; a green anole may often be seen on a weatherbeaten fence of a brown one hopping from one green leaf to another. The "disguise" appears to be of slight importance, and when it does occur is probably coincidental.

Color changes are actually brought about by temperature and light and the manner in which these factors influence the animal's activity and by emotional responses such as anger and fear. A low temperature induces a dark color whether the animal is in the shade or in the sun, but at a high temperature the color is subject to control by various factors. Darkness is generally accompanied by the green color, and shades of this same color are associated with fighting and other emotional excitement. The animal is also green when asleep and in death.

The Carolina anole is a delicate, slender little lizard that reaches a length of about six inches. The male is somewhat larger than the female and has a more highly developed fold of skin at the throat. This fold, the so-called dewlap, is dilatable into a "fan" and when fully expanded shows a bright raspberry red.

Strictly diurnal in habits, the anole does not rise with the sun but waits until the morning is well advanced and the temperature has risen. Then it leaves its customary perch, a horizontal twig well hidden among the leaves, on which it has passed the night and goes on the prowl for flies. It stalks the flies in the manner of a bird and captures them suddenly with a lightning thrust of its sticky tongue. The anole is quite at home among the trees, shrubs, and vines, running at ease among the branches, but being a natural acrobat, it often leaps from one leaf to another or to some other object to which it is able to cling by means of its adhesive foot pads.

All of us seem to know what a lizard is, and yet some of us often confuse a lizard with a snake or a salamander or even an earthworm. A lizard, in a word, is a cold-blooded animal with a moderately long body, usually ending with a tapering tail, and covered with a scaly skin. In size a lizard may range from the tiny gecko, which is little more than two inches long, to the komodo dragon, a large monitor lizard that measures more than ten feet in length. Most of the lizards in the United States are only a few inches long, an exception being the eastern glass lizard, which measures more than three feet.

Most lizards found in the United States occupy a rather limited area, though a few, such as the fence lizard, are fairly well distributed. This species occurs in two forms, the northern fence lizard and the southern fence lizard, and is found from southeastern New York to central Florida, and west to eastern Kansas and central Texas, the southern form being confined mostly to the coastal plain. The fence lizard, formerly known as the fence swift, belongs to a large and distinctive group of lizards known as the spiny lizards, or rough-scaled lizards, as their backs are covered with large, dull, keeled scales that terminate in sharp spinelike points. The male of the northern form is grayish brown with a series of poorly defined narrow, wavy, slightly darker crossbands on the back, and a broad, dark blue or gray area at the base of the throat. The sides of the belly are bright blue or greenish blue, bordered by black toward the center. The female tends to be grayer, with the crossbands on the back more distinct, and it has a whitish belly peppered with black. The southern form is similar but is slightly larger and with more brilliant markings.

The fence lizard is fairly common over much of the territory where it occurs. Its preferred habitat is dry, open, sunny woods, especially pine woods, where it may be found in such numbers as to suggest that these woods are its favored habitat. For this reason it is often called the pine lizard. It may be seen in piles of logs, brush heaps, and especially on fences. We frequently find it sitting on a fence post or running along a rail, hence its name. Though sometimes seen on the ground, it is quite adept at climbing, and thus trees and other objects on which it can climb are usually features of its environment.

When startled on the ground, it dashes for the nearest tree, climbs for a short distance, then moves to the opposite side, where it remains motionless. If we approach it from this side, it will climb still higher and again move to the opposite side, repeating this performance if necessary until it disappears from view among the branches.

Similarly, if surprised on a fallen log, it will dart to the opposite side, or if approached when on a fence, it will move to the opposite side and run along a rail for some distance, then stop and peer at us. Then if we move toward it, the lizard will repeat its previous behavior.

Of all our American lizards, the five-lined skink has possibly the widest distribution, being found throughout an area that extends roughly from southern New England to northern Florida and westward to southeastern South Dakota and central Texas. Thus anyone living in the eastern half of the United States can go into the woodlands and expect to see this lizard in its natural surroundings.

The five-lined skink prefers a somewhat moist but not wet environment and is generally found in wooded areas. Cut-over woodlots, with an abundance of rotting stumps and logs, abandoned sawdust piles, rock mounds, and masses of decaying debris usually harbor a specimen or two and are good places in which to look, though on a day when the temperature is high, we can often see it basking on a log or stump or stretched out in dry leaves on the ground. It is a nervous animal and when alarmed immediately scampers for cover; unlike other lizards, it does not run for a distance and then stop to peer back at an intruder. On a cool day it remains in some sheltered place, and when out foraging, it does not wander too far in search of food. Its diet consists of various small insects, earthworms, spiders, birds' eggs, and newly-born wood mice.

The color of the five-lined skink is highly variable, depending on age and sex. The young skinks measure up to four or five inches in length and have five white or yellowish stripes on a black ground and bright blue tails. They are often called the blue-tailed lizard, but as they grow older and larger, the pattern becomes less conspicuous—the stripes darken, the ground color lightens, and the tail turns gray. The females, as a rule retain some indications of the striped pattern. The males usually show traces of the stripes but tend to become nearly uniform brown or olive in color; in some parts of their range they develop an orange red pigment on their heads and thus are sometimes known as the red-headed skink. It is all somewhat confusing.

Unlike the secretive and wary skink, we can usually see the six-lined racerunner if we live within its quite extensive range (Maryland south to the Florida Keys, west to southeastern Wyoming, eastern Colorado, and Texas, and north in the Mississippi Valley to Lake Michigan, Wisconsin, and South Dakota) by merely going outdoors and visiting any one of its various habitats. It lives in fields, open woods, thicket margins, rocky outcrops, river flood plains, preferring dry places where the soil is loose or sandy and where there is plenty of cover in the form of stones, logs, boards, holes, or burrows—to be used as retreats during the night and on cool days.

On a warm sunny day we are likely to see many of these racerunners in such places as the species occurs in enormous numbers.

There is no mistaking this lizard, with its long, whiplike tail and its six light stripes that may be white, yellow, pale gray, or pale blue and extend from the head to the base of the tail.

The six-lined racerunner is an active species and rather bold, almost defiant at times. It will go about its business even though watched by an observer—if we keep our distance, about fifteen feet. But should we move a little closer, it will stop and watch us with a wary eye, and should we persist in moving still closer, it will scamper off and seek the nearest cover. If we are so foolhardy as to chase it, all we will have for our pains is to learn why it is called a racerunner, or "fieldstreak," as it is known in some parts of its range, for it can attain a speed of eighteen miles an hour.

It seems as if everyone has heard of the "horned toad" or, more accurately, the horned lizard. This curious-looking animal has been given considerable publicity over the years and is probably the best known of our American lizards with the possible exception of the Carolina anole.

We have some twenty-odd species of horned lizards. These flat, large-bodied, short-tailed, and grotesquely horned creatures are the most bizarre of all our lizards, or perhaps of all lizards. There are no others like them except for one odd species, the thorny devil, which occurs in Australia.

The horned lizards are western, terrestrial reptiles that occupy almost any type of flat, dry land where there is little or no vegetation. They are quite indifferent as to whether the soil is rocky, sandy, or loamy. In such places we can observe them darting here and there during the hottest part of the day. When they stop, they appear to have disappeared from sight because they blend so well with the substratum on which they live. They feed on spiders, sowbugs, and insects, especially ants, and they seem to require high temperatures to stimulate their appetite.

Long before sunset, even while the heat waves still shimmer above the ground, the horned lizards dig into the soil, where they spend the night, using their noses like plows and their heads like shovels. They may go two or three inches deep, or they may go only deep enough to cover their backs, with the heads just visible above the surface.

Despite their horns and cactuslike garb, with which most of them are adorned and which would appear to be ample protection, they are nevertheless preyed upon by such birds as the hawks and roadrunners and by such reptiles as the whipsnakes and collared lizards. When attacked, they puff themselves out into an almost flat shape, tuck their heads down, thus exposing the horns, and await the enemy.

The horned lizard is subject to a form of hypnotism. If we stroke it gently three or four times between the eyes, it will close its eyes and become very quiet, even losing some of its reflexes. But even more interesting, perhaps, is its habit of voluntarily ejecting a stream of blood from its eyes, to a distance of several feet.

Shrew
The perpetual eater

I am not quite sure that the word *perpetual* is the one to use in describing the eating habits of the shrew, for this tiny animal actually does not eat all the time. He comes close to it, however, for should he go without food for several hours, he would starve to death. It is amazing that he gets through the winter. His food, which consists essentially of insects, snails, and small annelids, would not seem to be sufficiently abundant to sustain him and to generate enough body heat to enable him to combat low temperatures. But apparently there are enough dormant insects to supply his needs, and also he can live on a plant menu for many days. Plants are eaten sparingly, though, and only if his preferred diet is unobtainable. Then, too, he will eat the dead bodies of larger animals whenever available.

The shrew, with his sleek fur, slender snout that always seems to be twitching, and delicate feet, is up and around during all hours and in all sorts of weather. But because of his small size, quick movements, and his habit of working under cover, we do not often see him. Occasionally, however, we might come upon him poking his delicate snout into crevices in the bark on the lower part of a tree trunk or ferreting about in the leaf mold or among decaying pieces of wood for his accustomed prey, or we might even see him dart from one shelter to another. More commonly we find his elfin tracks in the snow, sometimes in our own back yard.

Although the shrew will make his own runways, he does most of his traveling in the subsurface runways of other animals such as mice and moles. He is an extremely active animal, and because of his very rapid rate of digestion, he requires an enormous amount of food, eating at least his own weight in food each day merely to sustain life and commonly eating much more.

In spite of his small size (the common shrew measures barely four inches in length and weighs but four or five grams), he is a highly predatory, courageous, and pugnacious little animal and will not hesitate to attack creatures several times his own weight, such as mice.

I have never ceased to wonder how the shrew has been able to hold his own against a host of natural enemies and varying climatic conditions, since he ranges as far north as the Arctic Circle. How many shrews fall victim to the owls, hawks, shrikes, herons, foxes, and weasels that prey upon him with impunity can be seen by the large number of shrews' bones that are contained in owl pellets alone.

Yet the shrew is widely distributed and is abundant in many places. Perhaps one reason for his survival is that he is able to make his home wherever there is food and shelter, being as much at home in the dark, moss-carpeted forests of the north as in the deciduous woods and grassy fields and meadows farther south.

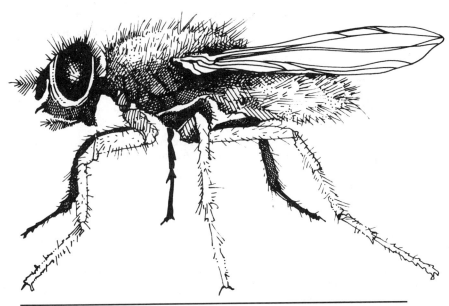

Flies

The ubiquitous pests

I think everyone will agree with me when I say that the best known and the most disliked of all animals is the house fly. And I might also add, perhaps the most dangerous, or potentially so, although recent methods of control and improved sanitation have reduced the house fly population in cities and towns and thus its potential of being a disease carrier.

The house fly, which hardly needs a description, has been called the typhoid fly with good reason; for although its favorite breeding place is horse manure, it will also breed in garbage and human excrement, where it is likely to pick up and thus transmit the germs of some thirty to forty different diseases, including typhoid, cholera, tuberculosis, and dysentery.

Should you wonder how it is capable of transporting the germs of such diseases, just look at its legs and body with a hand lens or magnifying glass. You will be astonished how thickly covered they are with hairs. It is in such growth that the dangerous microorganisms become lodged. But unless the hair tips are free from dust, they will not function too well; hence the fly always seems busy cleaning its feet by rubbing them against each other. You have doubtless seen the fly engaged in such a chore many times.

There have also been times when you have seen a house fly walk up a vertical pane of glass or across the ceiling upside down or on a wall and perhaps wondered how it was able to do so. Look between the claws on its feet, also with the magnifying glass, and you will find a pair of cushionlike structures. These cushions are provided with hollow hairs through which flows a sticky fluid that enables the fly to adhere to smooth substances. And while you still have the magnifying glass in your hand, look at one of the fly's eyes: It will look like a miniature golf ball. In other words, the outer surface of the *compound* eye is divided into a number of hexagonal areas, each one of which is the outer surface of a single eye. If you counted these smaller areas, you would find that each eye had four thousand of them. Is it any wonder, then, that the house fly can see us from almost any angle and so elude us with a facility that is often exasperating when we chase it with a swatter?

What makes a house fly of such importance, apart from its breeding habits and as a carrier of disease, is its reproductive capacity. If natural factors did not continually operate to keep the insect under control, the number of flies from one breeding pair in early spring would reach catastrophic proportions by late summer. For it has been estimated that a pair of these flies beginning operations in April might be the progenitors, if all were to live, of 191,010,000,000,000,000,000 by August.

There are all kinds of flies: dragonflies, mayflies, stone flies, scorpion flies, butterflies, fireflies, house flies, crane flies, flower flies, stable flies, robber flies. Only the last five are true flies in an entomological sense, a true fly being an insect with one pair of wings. Most insects have two pairs; a few do not have any. Presumably the true flies had two pairs at some remote time but lost the second pair through evolutionary processes and in place of the wings developed a pair of tiny, knobbed structures called halteres, which are organs of equilibrium. If one or both are removed, the fly can no longer maintain its equilibrium in the air.

There are some eighty-five thousand species of true flies, of which some fifteen thousand occur in North America. Some of us know a few of them as the crane flies, for instance, which we find in wet meadows and damp woods and by the brookside or along the edge of a pond. They look like overgrown mosquitoes, with narrow wings and long, slender legs that break off with the slightest provocation; to find a crane fly with its full complement of legs is something of a rarity. And speaking of mosquitoes calls to mind the midges, which resemble the mosquitoes and have been confused with them. They are small, fragile insects with long legs and slender wings and bodies. We usually see them in early spring and in autumn, generally near water, in dense swarms numbering sometimes in the millions, dancing in the air. They often make a distinct, rather loud humming sound. More than once I have inadvertently walked into a cloud of them. These midges are harmless, but not so the biting midges, which are real blood suckers. They are so small that we rarely see them, although we feel their bite when their needlelike pricks burn and sting. They are the pests that the Indians called the "no-see-ums," but they are probably better known as sand flies and punkies. They occur in shaded woods and fly both by night and during the day.

There are other biting flies, such as the black flies and deer flies. The black flies, which are also known as the buffalo gnats and turkey gnats, according to the parts of the country where they occur, are small insects with big, round eyes, stout bodies, humped backs, and short legs. Their bite can be very painful and is often accompanied by swelling, and their larvae have some rather interesting habits. The latter live among the rocks of a waterfall or in the rapids of a rushing stream, where they may be found by the thousands and collectively appear as a swaying mass of greenish black moss. They sit on their tails, as one writer has put it, clinging to a rock, stick, or leaf by means of a suction disc that is fringed with hooked hairs. Just behind the head is a fleshy proleg that is also provided with a sucker; so with these two suckers the larvae can move about with a sort of loping gait.

Of all these biting flies, I have found the deer flies the most vicious, inflicting a very painful bite that is usually accompanied by a swelling. They are about the size of a house fly, with wings that are banded or blotched, and are usually found near marshes and streams. They belong to the same family as the horseflies, of which there are several hundred different species in North America. The horseflies are black, brownish, or bluish with either clear or smoky wings. Rather large and robust, they are strong fliers, easily capable of outstripping a horse. Only the females bite—the males feed on nectar and sap from flowers and plants—and they are serious pests of horses, cattle, and other domesticated animals as well as deer and other large wild animals. Some species are guilty of transmitting certain diseases, such as tuleremia (rabbit fever) and anthrax.

From the time that the marsh marigolds blossom to late summer or early fall, we can see the brilliantly colored flower flies, probably the showiest and most attractive of all our flies, and so called because we usually find them on all kinds of flowers, where they feed on the nectar; as many of them are hairy, they are quite efficient pollinators. A number of these flower flies are well-known mimics of bees and wasps not only because of their color patterns but also because of their body form and habits; indeed, some even buzz.

Perhaps not quite as colorful as the flower flies and yet brightly colored with white, yellow, or red cross stripes on their abdomen are the soldier flies, so named because their colors resembled the somewhat gaudy uniforms that the soldiers of another day wore. They look much like wasps and like the wasps are more or less frequent visitors to various flowers, especially those of the carrot family. They are generally small, flat-bodied insects with short, wide or elongate tapered abdomens; in some species the abdomen is so wide that it extends on each side of the folded wings. And while we are on the subject of these gaily colored flies, we should also mention the peacock flies, small-to-medium-sized flies with a shining black, steely blue, or green body and black or brown spotted wings. They may be seen on flowers, fruits, and vegetables strutting about and waving their elevated wings back and forth as if to expose their beautiful wings and bodies to an admiring audience—hence their name.

On any summer's day we can see the robber flies flying about in open fields and swooping down upon any other flying insect, sometimes one as large as themselves, carrying it away to some convenient place where it can suck the victim's body juices at leisure. They are fairly large insects, generally with an elongate body and a very slender abdomen, though some species are quite stout and resemble bumblebees. The bluebottle and greenbottle flies are also much in evidence. Most of us know these metallic colored flies. They may often be seen about our garbage containers, and too frequently they enter our houses. These flies, or rather their larvae, perform a useful service as scavengers because they feed on dead animals and carrion. Most of us also know the tiny flies that so often fly about our fruit bowl or fruit basket. They are generally known as pomace flies or vinegar flies, having acquired the latter name because they usually gather about fruits or other plant materials that are fermenting or decaying. One of them, the red-eyed pomace fly, has become famous because of its use in the study of genetics.

There are many other flies including the moth flies, gall midges (one of which, the Hessian fly, is a destructive pest of wheat), snipe flies, cluster flies, bee flies, fruit flies (one of which, the Mediterranean fruit fly, was recently a major problem in California), grass flies, stable flies, flesh flies, and bot flies. And of course there is the mosquito, which is also a fly and a biting pest that sometimes torments us to no end, though it is only the female that bites.

Otter
The fish eater

Any armchair naturalist will tell you of the otter and its penchant for sliding, which most of us have read about. Few of us have actually seen the animal plunge down a steep slope, or even the animal himself, as he has secretive habits and is rarely observed. Anyone seeing an otter for the first time should have little difficulty in recognizing him, for his broad, flattened head, slender body, and tapering tail are good field marks. His short legs, webbed feet, and thick dense fur are also identifying characteristics.

   The otter is normally a playful animal and has a delightful sense of frivolity. Both the young and old will often engage in a game of tag, or tumble and wrestle, or play at follow-the-leader. An old female may play with a stone for hours at a time, tossing it from paw to paw or throwing it into the water and then diving after it, the object being to catch it before it reaches the bottom.

But the otter's favorite pastime is sliding. During the warmer months a number of otters will select a steep slope that drops into a stream or pond and then with feet turned backward will push off, going down on their bellies to plunge into the water. In winter they slide down a steep slope covered with ice and snow like small boys doing bellywhoppers on their sleds, the soft snow at the bottom acting as a sort of cushion to stop their downward plunge.

A family of otters, paddling about in the water or lying in the sun on a bank, is a picture of domestic tranquility. They converse in low, mumbling tones as they groom each other or engage in play, but if the play gets too rough, they will protest with a complaining whine or a sharp bark. A low warning grunt or cough is given as a signal of the approach of an enemy or other danger.

It is said that when the young, or pups, are old enough to be taught how to fend for themselves, the mother, who is a patient instructor, carries them on her back until they have lost their fear of water and only then will she teach them how to swim and to hunt for fish.

The otter has an individual range of many miles and is a great traveler but is usually not found far from a lake or stream except in winter when the water is frozen over. Then it becomes necessary to go overland in search of a hole in the ice or a pool kept open by cascading falls, for only in such places can the otter find the fish that is not only his favorite food but his mainstay at this season. The otter is an expert diver and graceful swimmer and can go long distances beneath the surface, as much as a quarter of a mile if necessary, before coming up for air.

The otter is unquestionably a competitor with humans for fish. It will eat fish in preference to other things but will also take crayfish, snails, frogs, insects, and the like when they are plentiful and easily secured. He is especially fond of salmon and trout but will prey on other species as well. The otter has a keen sense of smell and highly developed whiskers that serve as sense organs when searching for food in muddy waters. He is a cunning and stealthy fisher and will often creep slowly through the water to surprise some unwary fish, the fish always being swallowed head first and the tail discarded. After a meal, the otter usually cleans his face and whiskers by wiping them in the grass or snow.

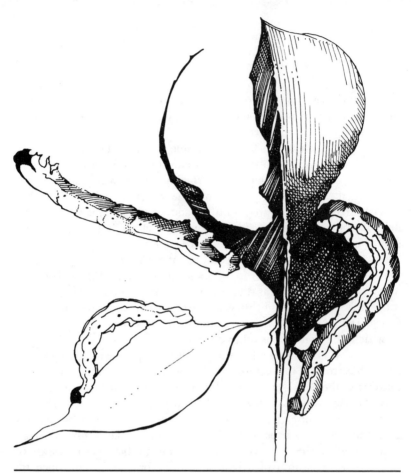

Measuring Worms
The earth measurers

Sometime during the spring we are likely to find in our back yard or garden as well as in fields, meadows, and woodlands small wormlike animals that move along over the ground or on a leaf or twig by a series of looping movements. We know them as measuring worms, inchworms, or spanworms—all these names being misnomers, as they are not worms but caterpillars—and just plain loopers. We also know them as geometers from the name of their family, which means earth measurers. There is an old saying that when they walk on our clothes they are measuring us for a new suit, which is as illogical as the idea that they are earth measurers. Anyway, if you want to know the reason for their peculiar locomotion, all you need do is examine one. You will find that since they have legs only at each end of the body, they have to hump themselves to get along.

There are some twelve hundred different species of these geometers in North America, but we don't see many of them. They look so much like twigs that we pass them by, or else they cover themselves with bits of the food they eat and thus become more or less invisible. Examine sometime a black-eyed Susan or a field daisy, and you will probably find in the flower head a collection of flower bits fastened to the back of one of these caterpillars.

When passing themselves off as twigs, they cling to a branch by their hind legs and hold their bodies out at an angle of about forty-five degrees, straight, stiff, and motionless. There are also many other details that promote the deception. Thus the legs that hold on to the stem partially surround the twig and appear to grow out of it, while the legs immediately behind the head are held close to the body. Likewise the head is often modified to suggest the top of the twig, and as a rule the color of the insect is in agreement with that of the twig, brown caterpillars selecting brown twigs, green caterpillars, green leaf stems.

You may well wonder how these caterpillars can hold their bodies out straight and stiff and remain motionless without becoming exhausted. There is no mystery about it, nor are the caterpillars endowed with special powers. They spin a thread of silk from their mouth and attach the free end to the twig at a point above that of contact. There is considerable tension upon the silken thread, for if it is severed, the caterpillars fall back with a sudden jerk.

Some of these measuring worms have the habit of letting themselves partway down to the ground by means of silken threads and then climbing back up in the manner of a sailor going up a rope. They might repeat this performance several times, but then comes the time when they lower themselves all the way to the ground and go into the earth, where they spin a tough, thin cocoon in which to pupate. They transform into small-to-medium-sized, slender-bodied, broad-winged moths that fly at dusk or at night and may often be seen around lights.

In one species, the fall cankerworm, the brownish gray moths emerge from their cocoons in the fall, and we often see them flying about like so many tiny ghosts in the bleak November woods. Only the males fly, as the females are wingless. But the females are not quite as sedentary as other wingless moths; as soon as they emerge from their cocoons they scramble up the trunks of trees, where they await the males. The eggs, which they fasten to the bark of the trees with a strong gluey secretion, are covered with gray hairs that they rub from their bodies. They look like tiny gray flowerpots arranged in somewhat irregular clusters, and they number several hundred.

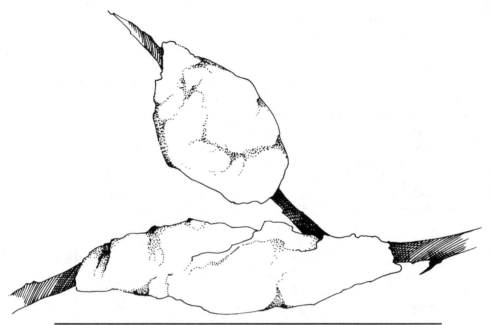

Freshwater Sponges
The pore bearers

In a previous chapter I remarked that the ordinary pond contains a vast assemblage of many kinds of animals and of plants, too, for that matter. I could also have added that practically every phylum of the animal kingdom (and of the plant kingdom) is represented, even the phylum Porifera, which includes the sponges. For the sponges are animals, a fact that may come as a surprise to many.

The famous Greek philosopher Aristotle was acquainted with the sponges and recognized them as animals, and so, too, did many others who followed him. True, there were some who viewed the sponges as plants and still others who considered them to be part animal and part plant. Anyway it was not until about 1870 or perhaps somewhat later that the question was finally settled.

Most of the sponges we use today are man-made synthetics; until a few years ago, when they came into general use, all of our sponges came from the sea, mostly in the form of the bath sponge, which many of us may recall. These sponges were the skeletal remains of marine animals.

Although sponges live principally in the sea, where they occur in many shapes and colors, some forty or more species are found in fresh water. These sponges are generally dull colored or greenish, and often mosslike, and usually cannot be seen in the water; even when seen, they are rarely recognized as sponges.

A sponge, whether a saltwater sponge or a freshwater sponge, consists of a number of animals living together in the form of a colony, a colony being a group of animals of the same species that are organically attached or held together. When seen with a magnifying glass or hand lens, a freshwater sponge is found to have a rough surface peppered with numerous holes, or pores; hence the name of the group, Porifera, which means pore bearing. The holes, or pores, which are of two sizes, are the openings of a network of canals and chambers through which water enters and leaves the sponge. The water enters through the small openings, called ostioles, passes through what are known as the incurrent canals and then into the chambers. From these chambers the water enters and passes through what are known as the excurrent canals and into a central cavity, called the gastral cavity, where it mixes with water from other canals. Finally the water passes out through the larger openings, called the oscula. The water is made to flow through the canals by briskly waving flagella (long whiplike processes, or extensions, of a cell or a single-celled animal) in the chambers (the flagellated chambers). It is in these chambers that food is removed from the water to feed the cells (animals) that make up the sponge, and it is in these chambers that the waste materials pass into the water, which eventually carries the waste out. Sponges can live only in clean water supplied with food and will quickly die should the water suddenly become polluted.

All sponges, whether marine or freshwater, have a latticelike framework, or skeleton, that functions as a support for the soft tissues, and which in the freshwater species is composed of small, transparent needles of silica. These needles, known as spicules, the largest of which measure about one hundredth of an inch, vary considerably in form. Thus they may be straight or curved, smooth or covered with brierlike points, or dumbbell shaped and sculptured, but whatever their form, they are always hooked or bound together in interlacing chains. Although sponges have spicules of various shapes, they are fairly constant for the species. Hence the spicules are a means of identification.

Although we do not readily see the sponges, or at least do not recognize them for what they are, they are quite abundant in lakes, ponds, pools, and clear slow-flowing streams. The sponges are not free-swimming but are always *sessile* (or stationed) on water-soaked logs, the leaves of submerged water plants, and the undersides of stones. Some species may branch out in slender, fingerlike processes, or extensions, that suggest plants in form as well as in color; other species may cover submerged twigs in spindlelike masses or be spread over stones in mats ten to fifteen inches in diameter and an inch or more thick at the center. Sponges that live where they receive considerable sunlight are frequently colored green by the small one-celled plants that live within them, whereas those that occur in the shade are a pale color. One of our more common species occurs on the surface of submerged logs, so if you want to find a sponge, your best chance is to look for a submerged log.

In the spring sponge colonies begin from small asexual units known as gemmules. The gemmules are little masses of living cells contained within a tough, hard, and highly resistant shell, which is provided with a pore through which the living cells can emerge in the spring to form new colonies. Once a colony has begun to form, it looks like a tiny fleck of white on a submerged leaf, stone, or log. Gradually it increases in size, reaching its maximum growth in July and August. Then in early fall it begins to shrivel and by October or November is dead. Meanwhile new gemmules—winter buds—have developed. Held among the interlocking spicules, they are the only parts of the sponge to live through the winter, as they are able to survive drying and freezing conditions. We can find the gemmules in autumn and throughout the winter, and we can see their general structure with a hand lens, though we need a microscope to examine the spicules.

Bumblebee
The hummer

Spring is always the time of great expectations and many surprises. We never know when we are to catch a glimpse of our first bluebird, robin, or phoebe, whose arrivals we so eagerly await, or when we shall find our first spring flower—perhaps the dainty hepatica hidden among the decaying leaves of the woodland floor or the delicate anemone of fragile beauty or even the common violet half hidden from the eye.

We may be thrilled at a glimpse of the first arrival from the South or by the discovery of some early blossom, but for some reason we take the appearance of the first bumblebee as a matter of fact, much as we take for granted the flowering of trees or the higher ascent of the sun in the sky. And yet to me, at least, the sight of a bumblebee flying low over a field or meadow in early spring is always a source of much delight, partly I suspect, because bumblebees have always fascinated me and partly because they prove an exception to the rule of "business before pleasure."

All of us are acquainted with the bumblebee in a sort of remote fashion, but few of us know that the bumblebees we see in early spring are the queens upon whom falls the duty of founding new colonies and perpetuating the species. They are the only survivors of last year's colonies, but how they manage to get through the winter is something we do not know. At any rate, they do not appear to be overly weighed down by the responsibility that Nature has entrusted to them. If they were, it would seem that they would be anxious to get to work and establish new colonies before anything happened to them. But before settling down to more serious matters, they fly about and enjoy themselves, sipping the nectar of early flowers and filling the bags on their hind legs with pollen grains.

Such activity, however, is not without purpose, for after a fast of eight or nine months they must store up energy in preparation for their domestic duties. Furthermore, they must obtain the food necessary to feed the growing grubs of the new colony.

At last, having filled the bags on their hind legs with pollen grains and now feeling fit to get to work, they begin to look about for a suitable place in which to fashion their nests. They search carefully and diligently for some abandoned nest of a field mouse or chipmunk, usually underground, but if they are unable to find one they will appropriate a bird's nest.

Having selected a suitable site, the queen now mixes the pollen and nectar she has gathered into a loaf about the size of a bean and places it on the floor of the nest. On this mass, or "beebread," she lays a few tiny eggs and covers them with wax that she exudes from between her abdominal segments. Then she proceeds to fashion a thimblelike honey pot, which she fills with honey to serve as food while she broods over the eggs. Upon emerging from the eggs, the larvae, or grubs, feed on the beebread under the waxen coverlet, which the queen pierces from time to time so that the grubs may have access to the food. As they feed, the grubs burrow deeper and deeper into the beebread, each one making a sort of cave for itself. In about a week or so, the grubs become full grown at which point each one spins a thin, papery but tough cocoon in which it pupates. The queen then broods on the cocoons and sips from her honey pot.

About ten days or two weeks later, the grubs emerge as

adult bumblebees. They are smaller than the queen and are called workers for upon them fall the tasks of gathering more nectar and pollen and adding it to the mass of beebread and of helping to rear other workers. Henceforth the queen devotes her entire time to laying eggs. Later the workers strengthen the silken pupa cradles with wax and convert them into cells for storing honey.

The first generation of workers is followed by others, which we see during the spring and summer flying about over the fields and meadows and visiting the orchards and gardens. They are collecting nectar and pollen, so often seen hanging in golden masses from their hind legs. The pollen grains are transported in the so-called pollen baskets, which are smooth, shining hollows on the outer surface of the hind legs, with long, overhanging hairs on the sides. If we listen carefully as we watch these bumblebees going about their chores, we will hear them humming. It was this humming that gave them the name of bumblebee, from the Middle English word *bumblen*, which meant "to hum."

As one generation is followed by another, the colony gradually increases in size until the climax is reached in late summer, when young queens and males are produced. Then as summer wanes, the workers begin to die off. They are soon followed by the males, which die after they have performed their marital duties. The mother queen, having fulfilled her destiny, also dies, leaving only the young queens to find some cosy retreat in which to spend the winter. This is usually in the ground, from two inches to a foot below the surface, each queen by herself.

Bumblebees collect nectar and pollen for their own use and in all likelihood do not realize the benefit they confer on the flowers they visit. In fact, many flowers are quite dependent upon their insect visitors for pollination and could not set seed without them. The red clover, for instance, is unable to do so without the aid of the bumblebees, for they are the only insects with tongues long enough to reach the nectar. There is the classic story of how the Australians imported quantities of red clover for fodder and had a bountiful crop the first year but not a single seed for the following year's crop because they had neglected to import bumblebees.

Fairy Shrimp
The disappearing act

One of the most mysterious animals that I know of is the fairy shrimp, one reason being that I never know where I'll find it. I might find it in a certain pool one year and then return to the same pool the next year or the year after, and even the year after that, and look for it in vain; I might also look in a neighboring pool, which to all appearances is exactly like the first, and not find it there. But next year I might find the animal in this second pool but not in the first, and yet again I might find it in both pools. For several years the fairy shrimp may appear in the same pool as regularly as the seasons and then not be seen there for four or five years, even though the conditions appear to be the same. Moreover, one species may be present in one pool and a quite different species in a pool close by. In short, the appearance and distribution of the fairy shrimp is freakish and sporadic, and anyone finding it, at least for the first time, can record the event as a red-letter day.

In spite of its name, the fairy shrimp is not a shrimp, though it is distantly related to the shrimps and resembles them in form. It is a small animal, measuring only about an inch long, though sometimes it may reach a length of four inches. It is semitransparent and is colored with iridescent tints of red, blue, and green, which contrast with the shimmering bronze of the leaflike appendages that are used to propel it through the water. Altogether not an unattractive animal.

Unlike most swimming animals, the fairy shrimp always swims on its back, which is so transparent that it is possible to see the beating of its tubular heart. It is unusually graceful as we watch it dart through the water, then drift lazily along for a moment or so, and then suddenly dart forward again.

There are eleven pairs of leaflike appendages, or leaf feet, as they are called, and they are borne on the body segments posterior to the head; when the animal is swimming, they are pressed back against the water, each pair in succession, in a series of wavelike movements. Thus, when the animal is swimming, the waving plumes of the leaf-feet become the conspicuous part of the fairy shrimp, though hardly less so than the rich colors that shimmer in the sunlight.

The leaf feet not only serve to propel the fairy shrimp through the water but also are used in respiration and hence are really gill feet. Accordingly, as the fairy shrimp glides through the water, currents of water pass back over the gill feet, and at the same time a single current of water is drawn forward along the center of the body between the pairs of gill feet. This current of water contains microscopic food, such as protozoans, diatoms, rotifers, and bits of detritus, on which the animal feeds. The food is filtered out of the water in a sort of food trough between the "chewing bases" of the gill feet and conveyed to the mouth by their movements.

Fairy shrimps occur in early spring in small, often temporary pools formed by melting snow or ice or by rain. They seem to appear suddenly and somewhat miraculously, almost overnight, I might say, and they mature and reproduce within a few short weeks.

Adult fairy shrimps, spiderlike young (called nauplii), recently emerged from eggs, and maturing young larvae may all be found swimming together in the cold water. As this is the mating season, many pairs may be observed swimming about together, always on their backs, the male above the female, the two in close embrace. We can easily distinguish the sexes—the male by his modified antennae, called claspers, which he uses to hold the female, and the female by her prominent brood pouch. Just behind the gills, on the eleventh segment of the body, are tubelike appendages by which the male transfers the sperm cells to the female. In all species of fairy shrimps, the females appear to be much more abundant than the males; as a matter of fact, in some species there are no males, the young developing from eggs that have never been fertilized by male cells (parthenogenesis).

Fairy shrimps can live only in cold water, and therefore mating has to be accomplished without much loss of time, within a matter of a few weeks. Then as the water begins to warm up, the adults fall to the bottom and die but not before the females have released their eggs, which also fall to the bottom. The eggs eventually hatch into nauplii (an immature stage with three pairs of appendages), which will undergo several molts before becoming adult. As a rule, the eggs will not hatch until sometime in late winter, lying dormant in the mud throughout the summer and fall. But as they are sensitive to temperature changes, they may hatch in the fall, when young fairy shrimps are sometimes found in pools during mild weather after a very early autumn freeze. That may serve to explain why the distribution and appearance of these animals is freakish and irregular—in the pools where young may be observed in the autumn, few, if any, will be seen the following spring.

Mayflies
The death dance

During the months of May and June we are likely to see the mayflies around our porch lights and on our window screens. Look at them closely and you will see that they are beautiful, fragile insects, soft gray and brown or pale and translucent, with large front wings and small hind ones and with two or three long tails that extend backward from the tip of the body.

These mayflies were but a short time ago *naiads* (young mayflies) that lived in the water until reaching their full growth. They then crawled out of the water and onto the stems and leaves of water plants, to which they attached themselves. Shortly thereafter their skin split down their backs and they emerged not as fully developed adults but as subadults, a stage unique to the life cycle of the mayflies and one that may last from a few minutes to several days. During this stage, which is one of inactivity, the legs and tail filaments elongate and the reproductive system develops to maturity. At length, the entire skin of the subadults is shed, and the now fully developed mayflies take to wing. Quite frequently clouds of these flying insects may be seen in the vicinity of a pond or stream, but as they are attracted to lights, they often venture some distance from the ponds and streams, and we may see them flying by the hundreds around a single street lamp and in fewer numbers around our own porch lights.

Most of these insects live only a few hours, or at the most, a day or two, although a few species live several weeks. There is no way for them to live longer because they are unable to eat. Their mouth parts are shrunken, if not actually vestigial, and useless, and their digestive tract has been transformed into a sort of balloon that is inflated with air and helps them to fly. Furthermore, their legs are delicate structures and not well adapted for walking.

All this is for a purpose: Their main objective in life is to mate, and once mating has taken place and the females have deposited their eggs in the water, they all die. Sometimes the surface of ponds and streams are strewn with their bodies—which become food for eager fishes—and so are the streets and sidewalks of nearby towns and villages.

There are few phenomena of the insect world more striking than the mating flight of these insects. It usually occurs in the cooler hours of the day or in the evening just after sunset. Thousands may participate in the mating flight, swinging up and down through the air in a joyous, rhythmic dance, which might just as well be called the dance of death. They move up and down together, swinging downward in a swift descent toward the surface of the pond or stream and then bounding upward as if they were thistledown wafted by a gentle breeze.

Most of them die an heirless death, for there are many males but few females. The latter lay their eggs almost immediately. The short-lived species deposit them in clusters that rapidly disintegrate upon reaching the water, whereupon the eggs sink to the bottom; the less perishable species drop the eggs one at a time. The females of these species either alight on the surface of the water at intervals to wash off the eggs or creep down into the water, enclosed within a film of air, to lay them on the undersides of stones and then float up to the surface and fly away. We should not feel sorry for these insects, believing that they live for only a few hours. Actually the naiads live for several years; and as matter of fact, the mayflies live longer than most insects, although their life span is certainly exceeded by some wood-boring beetles that take as long as ten years to mature and by the periodical cicada that takes even longer.

We can easily recognize the mayfly naiads by their long bodies, with their two or three long tail filaments that may be fringed and fernlike, and by their paired abdominal gills. They occur in many shapes and sizes, according to the species, and have different habits. Thus, some swim about in the water, others run actively over the bottom, still others merely creep. Some sprawl in the mud, others burrow in it. Some are found in ponds, others in quiet pools, and still others in flowing rivulets or tumbling waterfalls. They are herbivorous for the most part, feeding on algae, diatoms, and other vegetation, though some are known to feed at times on other aquatic insects.

Bullfrog
A jug of rum

If you have never heard the bullfrog call in his deep bass voice on an early summer's evening, you have missed what is probably one of the most, if not *the* most, unusual calls of a wild animal. If we hear it suddenly and unexpectedly, we may be momentarily stunned as it falls upon our ears. The call, which somewhat resembles the roar of a bull at a distance, though it has a more musical ring, has been variously interpreted as "be drowned," "better go 'round," "blood 'n' ouns," "br-wum," "knee deep," "bottle-o'-rum," "more rum," and "jug-o'-rum," the last probably the most accurate and the most common interpretation.

If we stand on the shore of a pond from which the call issues and try to pinpoint its source, we will have little success if the frog is some distance out in the pond. If, however, he is near at hand, then we are likely to see him lying submerged among the water weeds, his head above the surface of the water and his eyes glittering in the twilight like two big beads.

Our largest frog, with adults measuring as much as seven to eight inches in length, the bullfrog is found from the Canadian border south to central Florida, west to Wisconsin and Nebraska, and south through the Great Plains. In color he is green or greenish brown with white slightly mottled underparts and yellow on the throat, especially in the males. In the southeastern part of his range, he is usually very dark, being heavily patterned with dark gray or dark brown. Some are almost black above and heavily mottled below. We may easily distinguish the bullfrog from other frogs, whatever his size. His head is broad and flat, his ears are much larger than his eyes, and he lacks any lateral folds, although there is a short fold of skin extending backward from his eye, over his ear, and down to his shoulder. We might also add that his hind feet are fully webbed, with the fourth toe protruding well beyond the others.

The bullfrog prefers large ponds or lakes fringed with low willows, alders, and other water-loving trees and shrubs, where the water is both deep and shallow, and where there are sheltering growths of pickerelweed, arrowhead, and water lilies. These growths serve as good hiding places, and around the roots and stems and beneath the leaves, may be found crayfish, water beetles, water bugs, snails, shrimps, the larvae of dragonflies, and the naiads of mayflies, which form his diet.

The bullfrog is strictly an aquatic species, by which we mean that he lives in the water throughout his entire life. Unlike the leopard frog and the pickerel frog, he will rarely hunt for food in any place other than in the pond that serves as his home. We should never expect to see him in a field or meadow or orchard, even though such places may be near a pond or lake, unless we have had a continuous heavy rain for some time. After such a rain, we may find him out of his pond on a hunting expedition or perhaps migrating from one pond to another. In spite of his heavy body, he can move over the ground in a series of leaps of five or six feet in length, leaving in the wet sand or mud a somewhat curious track that shows a large part of the lower surface of his body and his thighs with his front feet toeing in.

I have often stood by the edge of a pond to observe the many forms of animal life to be found in it, and I recall one time when the shadow of a hawk suddenly appeared on the surface of the water. Before I realized what was happening, the bullfrog that had been resting on a lily pad suddenly dived into the water and swam quickly to a place of safety among the water weeds. The bullfrog is a powerful swimmer, as we might expect from the size and length of his hind legs, but when swimming, he always keeps his eyes closed to protect them against the swift passage through the water. But by doing so he has to stop or at least slow down after swimming a short distance, to get his bearings. That makes him vulnerable to any enemy, and if one is near at hand, he again dives and resumes his swimming. Sometimes, though, he does get caught.

When underwater the bullfrog does not use his lungs in breathing; his nostrils are always kept closed, and his throat does not show any of the swallowing movements that are so much in evidence when breathing air. Moreover, his moist skin is like a giant gill. Thus he can live under water for months at a time; as a matter of fact, he often, by preference, will lie on the bottom of a pond with flattened body and closed nostrils.

The bullfrog is solitary in habits, except during the mating season, and you will never hear him participating in a chorus. He is the last of our frogs to emerge from hibernation and in the North will not begin to breed until about the last of June or in July, when the air temperature is about 80 degrees and the water temperature has warmed to 70 degrees; in the South he breeds much earlier. During the breeding period the frogs may be seen floating partly outstretched on the surface of the pond or lake, and should we play a flashlight on them at night, they will appear to be momentarily paralyzed.

The eggs, which are small and black and white, are laid in masses numbering from ten thousand to twenty thousand, and are anchored to plant stems, more or less hidden by the plant growth. The tadpoles, olive in color with fine specks of black, require two years or more to transform into adult frogs, thus spending two winters and sometimes a third in the tadpole stage before completing their transformation in late August. Any tadpoles we see swimming about in the ponds in late fall or early spring are those of either the green frog or the bullfrog, the latter if they are more than three and a half inches long.

Bullfrogs hibernate in the mud of ponds and lakes, where the tadpoles also spend the winter. Tadpoles have been reported to be active throughout the winter in several of the central and southern states; in some places they have been seen swimming near holes in the ice.

The legs of the bullfrog are a gourmet's delight.

Box Turtle
The boxed

As we have previously remarked, when most of us think of turtles we usually think of those we find in the ponds and streams. These are the ones we commonly see. But there are several species that are more or less terrestrial in habit and that we generally refer to as land turtles, as opposed to the water forms. We have already met one of them, the wood turtle, and we are now about to become acquainted with another, the box turtle, which is found over nearly all of the eastern half of the United States. But even this turtle, which was once described as strictly terrestrial, often takes to water, especially during the hot, dry spells of summer, when it seeks a muddy or watery place and soaks in the water or mud for hours at a time; at such times it will often fall into a deep sleep, which appears to be a form of aestivation.

We can easily recognize the box turtle by its high domed shell and we can even distinguish the sexes by the color of their eyes. Those of the male are red or sometimes pink; those of the female are normally brown, though at times they may be purplish or grayish. The box turtle is so called because it is able to box itself in when alarmed or when threatened with danger. Its lower shell (plastron) is divided crosswise, the two parts being fastened together by a hinge of cartilage. By means of a strong set of muscles, the upper and lower shells can be closed together so neatly and so powerfully that it is extremely difficult, if not impossible, to pry them apart. They fit so closely that not even a knife blade can be inserted between them. Hence the entire shell provides adequate protection against all predatory animals, though sometimes some of the turtles become so fat from gluttony that they cannot completely withdraw within the shell. They are then exposed to attacks by rats and other predatory animals.

Adult box turtles measure from four and a half to six inches in length; a few thousand years ago they were considerably larger, and even today an extraordinarily large specimen may occasionally be found in northern Florida. The entire shell is covered with horny plates about as thick as a thumbnail and extremely variable in coloration and pattern from one part of its range to another; hence we have several subspecies. Both upper and lower shells may be yellow, orange, or olive on a black or brown ground color, and either dark or light colors may predominate. In the male, which is commonly the larger of the two sexes, the rear lobe of the lower shell has a central concave area; in the female the lower shell is flat or slightly convex. The turtle's head is rather small, the snout ending in a sort of overhanging beak, which in some subspecies is notched. In the young turtles the shell is much flatter, mostly a grayish brown, and each large plate has a spot of yellow.

The box turtle is essentially a land turtle and primarily a woodland species but often wanders into fields, meadows, and open areas adjacent to woods. In hilly regions, it prefers hillsides and other upland places, though it seems equally at home in flat country. When the temperature is high, it craves a certain amount of moisture and will seek a muddy or watery place. If unable to find such a place, it will burrow beneath a log or in rotting vegetation; a summer shower will invariably bring it out of hiding. During the hot summer months we are more likely to find the box turtle in a densely shaded area along a stream where it will sometimes enter the water and float with its head and upper third of its domed shell above the water. It may even occasionally swim beneath the surface but with less facility than the strictly aquatic species with their flatter shells.

The box turtle lives a more or less solitary life and spends most of its time within a rather well defined area. The radius of its home territory is usually less than 750 feet, though it may be as much as half a mile. Within this area the turtle wanders at random but with a strong sense of direction. It is most active just after sunrise and just before sunset as well as during a warm rain. At night it burrows into the leaf mold.

The box turtle, though essentially a vegetarian, includes in its diet a variety of animals, such as the larvae of insects, slugs, snails, caterpillars, and earthworms. It is inordinately fond of blackberries and gorges on them in late summer. There are times when it may appear in our garden to feast on tomatoes.

Mating usually occurs in the spring and fall, though breeding may take place any time during the period when the turtle is active. The male turtle at such a time will follow the female about, sometimes lunging at her, at other times pushing her, and occasionally even biting her until she succumbs to his advances.

When mating has been consummated, the female excavates a flask-shaped cavity in soft soil, beginning her task, which usually takes from three to five hours, in late afternoon or early evening. On finishing her digging, the female then deposits in the cavity three to four, though sometimes as many as eight, white elliptical eggs, which are roughly one and a quarter inches long and three-quarters of an inch in diameter, and then fills the cavity with earth, packing it down by treading over it. Occasionally before leaving the site of her eggs, she voids the contents of her bladder over it. In short, she conceals the site so well that it is virtually invisible.

Carpenter Ants
The carpenters

There was the time when I was visiting a friend of mine, and while standing on the front porch where I was taking my leave, I happened to notice a number of ants running over the floor and disappearing into a hole in the base of one of the wooden columns that supported the roof of the porch. I called my friend's attention to them and suggested he do something about them before he got into serious trouble—if he was not already in serious trouble. I found out later that he had to replace the entire column.

Much has been written about ants, and most of us are acquainted with them in a general way, so it seems hardly necessary to say much about them. Yet a few words might not be amiss. The ants are small-to-medium-sized insects readily recognized by the form of their body and by the narrowed, modified front part of the abdomen known as the pedicel that consists of one or two segments and bears a knob, swelling, or an upright scale. There are more than thirty-five hundred species. They occupy almost every conceivable type of habitat and outnumber all other land animals. In color they may be black, brown, reddish, or yellowish and may be either somewhat hairy or completely naked. Some species have a sting, and many of them are able to secrete a powerful burning acid. In feeding habits, they are carnivorous, herbivorous, or omnivorous; in short, some prey on other animals, others live on seeds or fungi, and still others are general scavengers. A few are even parasitic on the gleanings of other ants. They are especially fond of the honeydew secreted by other insects, such as the aphids, and some species even tend the aphids in much the same way as farmers tend to their cattle.

The ants are gregarious by nature and live together in what are known as colonies; hence they are considered social insects. A colony, which may contain as few as a dozen individuals or as many as a million or more, consists of one fertile female—the queen—infertile females, the workers and soldiers, and some other specialized castes. Usually there are males and other fertile females only once a year. The sole function of the queen is to lay eggs, and after just one mating with a male, she can lay fertile eggs continuously for as long as she lives, which may be as long as twenty years. The function of the workers, whose life span may be ten years or more, is to maintain the colony by performing all the necessary chores and duties essential to its welfare; and that of the soldiers, which are modified workers, is to safeguard the colony from intruders and strangers and from attacks by various enemies.

As a rule, the colony is established by the queen alone, though occasionally she must have the assistance of the workers of the same species or of other species. She founds the colony after the nuptial flight during which the winged males and winged fertile workers mate. After mating the males die, and the impregnated females, or queens, chew off or scrape off their wings. Then each digs a hole in the soil or under a stone or piece of bark, seals herself in it, and waits for the ripening of her eggs, which will occur within a few weeks. The young, or larvae, that emerge from the eggs are fed by saliva from the queens' mouth. They develop into small, undernourished workers, upon whom devolve the duties of feeding the queen, enlarging the nest, and taking care of the second brood of young. Thereafter, successive broods of workers engage in maintaining the colony.

The ants I saw running over the floor of my friend's porch were the black carpenter ants, a name well taken because they are black in color and they work in wood. They are our largest ants, the workers being about three-eighths of an inch long, the queen about an inch, the males somewhat shorter, and they are a common species throughout the eastern half of the United States. Unlike other ants, which build their nests in soil, in sand, or in living plant tissues, the black carpenter ant builds its nest in the dead wood of living trees, in logs, fence posts, and telephone poles, and in the timbers of buildings. Its nest consists of a series of anastamosing galleries and chambers, which it excavates in the wood, but unlike the termites it does not eat the wood itself. It often gets into our houses, and we see it wandering about on the floors or crawling about on the kitchen sink in search of sweets or other food. It is more of a nuisance than anything else unless it takes to building its nest in the timbers or woodwork, when it can become quite destructive. As a matter of fact, an extensive nest or colony of these ants may so weaken a building that it can very well collapse.

Sometimes a rove beetle finds its way into the nest of the black carpenter ant and becomes a more or less permanant resident. This beetle, which we know by the name of *atemeles*, has tufts of yellow hairs on the sides of its abdomen and beneath. These are glands that secrete a substance that the ants appear to be very fond of, as a matter of fact, so fond that the ants care for the beetle almost as we would care for a pet, keeping it clean and feeding it. Even the larvae of the beetle are fed along with the ants' own larvae. And what is most surprising is that if the ant's nest is broken into, the ants will rush to the defense of the beetle's larvae in preference to their own.

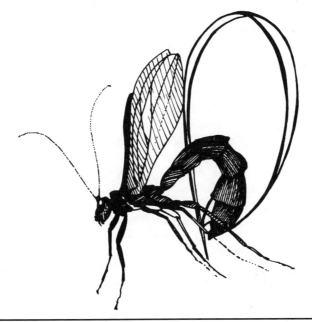

Ichneumon Flies
The seekers

According to Webster, the word *ichneumon* comes from a Greek word that literally means "a tracker." Our use of the word today, both in a scientific and popular sense, is derived from the name of the so-called Egyptian ichneumon, which was a mongoose (*Herpestes ichneumon*) considered sacred by the ancient Egyptians because it was supposed to devour the eggs of the crocodile. The name is applied to a group of insects known as the ichneumon flies because they seek out the larvae of other insects, especially caterpillars, in which to lay their eggs. The eggs are laid on, near, or beneath the skin of the larvae, on which their young are to feed. These ichneumon flies are not, strictly speaking, flies in an entomological sense and perhaps might be more accurately called ichneumon wasps, as they more or less resemble the wasps.

The ichneumons are usually regarded as parasitic, but technically they might better be considered parasitoids (a parasitoid is intermediate in habits between a parasite and a predator) or predaceous, as they eventually kill their victims. There are some six thousand species in the United States, but the group is so large and complex and the species so often resemble each other that it really requires an expert to identify them. Entomologists, of course, are well acquainted with them, but most of us are not, except perhaps for a few species. Yet they are common enough and may be seen during the warmer months of the year flying about in the fields and woods, even in our gardens and back yards, or wherever insects are to be found except in the ponds and streams.

The ichneumon flies are mostly small or medium-sized slender insects, though some are fairly large. They have an elongate abdomen, which is rather sickle shaped in about half the species and cylindrical in others, very long and threadlike antennae and comparatively large wings, though the females of some species are wingless. Many of the females have an ovipositor, which is an organ, or device, for laying eggs. In most cases it protrudes from the tip of the body and is often twice as long as the body. The ovipositor enables the females to reach larvae that live in burrows deep in the trunks of trees. When the eggs hatch, the young feed on the tissues and juices of the host, usually burrowing within its body, and eventually causing its death. Millions of ichneumon flies labor constantly in an effort to keep under control various destructive insect pests and thus are of considerable value. Unfortunately, they also attack beneficial species.

Of the many species of ichneumon flies, the ones we are most likely to recognize as ichneumons are those that belong to the genus *Magarhyssa*. They are the largest and have ovipositors from two to four or five inches long. They are parasitic on the wood-boring larvae of the sawflies, a group of insects whose ovipositor is often somewhat sawlike, and they are particularly parasitic on the genus *Tremex*, whose members are generally known as horntails because the last abdominal segment bears a more or less hornlike prolongation.

Like the ichneumons, the female horntails also have an ovipositor, which they use to drill a hole in a tree in which they deposit an egg. This egg hatches into a small grub, which makes a small burrow as it feeds on the tissues of the tree. If lucky, the grub will feed and grow and finally emerge from its burrow as an adult horntail, but more likely it will be parasitized by an ichneumon.

Should we stroll through the woods during the summer, we are very apt to see one of the species of *Megarhyssa*, perhaps *magarhyssa lunator*, popularly known as the lunate long-sting, flying about or exploring the trunk of a tree for one of the horntails, especially the species known as the *pigeon tremex*. The long-sting, incidentally, may be easily recognized by the yellow, brown, and gray stripes on her body.

If we watch her carefully, we will see her tap a given area gently with her antennae, moving back and forth, and then suddenly fasten the claws of her feet in the bark. Next she raises her abdomen upward on her widely stretched legs, making a sort of derrick with her body, and then places the tip of her ovipositor directly below the tip of her abdomen. As the ovipositor is too long to be held vertically, the female coils the excess length into a sack formed by the last two abdominal segments, which are quite membranous, the sack eventually resembling a thin, transparent, flattened balloon.

At last she is ready to drill. Slowly but steadily the ovipositor begins to pierce the wood, for at the tip are tiny teeth that saw the wood fibers apart. After some drilling, she finally reaches the burrow of the *pigeon tremex* and in it deposits an egg. Immediately on hatching, the larva of the long-sting begins to feed on the occupant of the burrow, eventually destroying it but not before it has become fully grown. It then pupates, and when fully developed, the adult ichneumon gnaws its way through the bark, emerges through a hole in it, and takes to wing. How the female long-stings can locate the burrows of the *pigeon tremex*, or for that matter, how any of the other species of *Megarhyssa* can locate the burrows of the sawflies on which they lay their eggs is still a mystery.

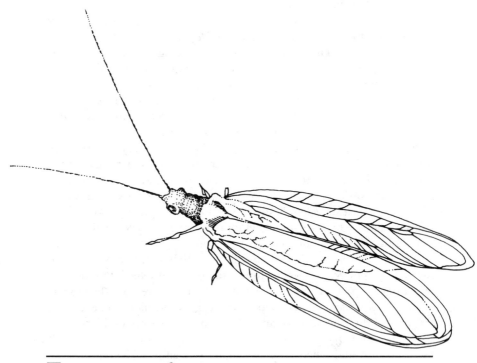

Lacewing
A study in contrasts

Few of us have given much thought, if any, to the way insects lay their eggs. If we did, we would soon discover that the urge to safeguard their eggs and to make ample provision for their young is so strong in many species that they have developed unusual habits to ensure their survival. Let us consider, for instance, the golden-eyed lacewing. It is a dainty and delicate little insect with long hairlike antennae, green, gauzy wings, and iridescent golden eyes, quite common during the warm days of summer. We see it flying about in our gardens, in fields and meadows, along the roadside, or sitting on some leaf with its wings held rooflike over the sides of its body.

When the female lacewing is ready to lay her eggs, she

selects a leaf that supports a colony of aphids or plant lice, and on the surface of the leaf she places a drop of a sticky fluid that she ejects from the tip of her body. Then she lifts up her slender abdomen and spins the tiny drop into a thread half an inch or more long, which quickly hardens on exposure to the air into a stiff stalk. She next lays an oblong egg about the size of a pinhead on the tip of the stalk. The egg firmly in place, she places another drop of the sticky fluid on the surface of the leaf, spins it into a thread as long as the first, and when it hardens into a stiff stalk, she lays a second egg on the tip. She repeats this performance a number of times until she has laid her full complement of eggs.

The young, or larvae, that emerge from the eggs are quite unlike the dainty and beautiful adult insect. They are queer-looking creatures, with extremely large heads. The sides of the spindle-shaped body are armed with immense curved hairs that give them a ferocious appearance, and they have long, pointed, sickle-shaped jaws, which are effectual instruments for grasping soft-bodied aphids. The jaws also form a hollow tube with an opening at each end, the opening at the base leading into the animal's throat, so they also serve as an efficient sucking apparatus.

Like the praying mantis, they are predatory to a high degree, but like the mantis, they confine themselves to feeding chiefly on aphids, and for that reason are called aphis lions. They always seem hungry and will devour their own brothers and sisters as quickly as any other insect.

So here we have the reason why the mother lacewing lays her eggs on stalks. If she laid them side by side or in a mass on the leaf, the first aphis lion to emerge from the egg would probably take to eating the eggs. If several emerged at the same time, they would probably eat one another, as spiderlings do when they hatch within the egg case. So what does she do? She places the eggs beyond reach.

That leaves nothing for the newly emerged aphis lion but an inedible stalk, and as there is no place to go but down the stalk, the hungry insect grasps the stalk with its first pair of legs and with the help of the other two pairs begins a careful descent. This is quite a feat for a creature only a few minutes old and with no previous experience at gymnastics. At last it arrives safely on the leaf and pauses for a moment to look around. It could, of course, ascend one of the neighboring stalks and feed on one of its unhatched brothers or sisters, but spying the nearby aphids, it proceeds to satisfy its hunger without further ado.

It is surprising the number of aphids an aphis lion will consume; it almost seems that the number it will consume is limited only by the number available. Try counting the number of aphids an aphis lion will eat at one sitting and you will probably tire of the exercise before the aphis lion does. When full grown, the aphis lion spins a white spherical cocoon, usually on the lower surface of a leaf. Later the winged adult escapes through a circular hole that it cut before transforming. The piece cut out remains attached to the rim of the hole like a lid.

Summer Birds
Summer visitors

After the first early spring arrivals of the bluebird, robin, phoebe, and redwing, there follows an almost daily succession of other migratory birds so that by the time spring passes into summer, we see and hear birds everywhere: in the fields and meadows, in the marshes and swamps, in the woodlands, thickets, and orchards, in the vicinity of ponds and streams, and even in our garden and about our house. I have often had a chipping sparrow nest in a tree in my back yard and more than once have been awakened in early dawn by his reiterated chipping, the little brown-capped sparrow being an early riser. On occasion I have had as a visitor the ruby-throated hummingbird, an exquisite little mote of a bird and in many respects a most remarkable one.

It is somewhat unusual for the chipping sparrow to nest

near the habitation of man. To be sure, we also find it in meadows, where we also find the vesper sparrow, the Savannah sparrow, and the grasshopper sparrow. The last is not named because of its fondness for grasshoppers, though it is not averse to eating these insects, but rather because of its grasshopperlike attempt at singing—if we can call it singing. Moreover, it is so persevering in trying to give voice to a melody that it not only sings during the day but will even awaken at night to sing.

Unlike these sparrows, the swamp sparrow prefers the swamp and marshes as a nesting site, as does also the pied-billed grebe, the red-winged blackbird, the Virginia rail, the sora, and both the least bittern and the American bittern, all of which we can find should we care to visit such a place. I can distinctly recall the first time I saw the American bittern. If the bird had not moved, I would never have seen it because it can assume at times a posture that so closely resembles a stump root projecting from the water as to be passed by unnoticed. To see the long-billed marsh wren we will have to find a cattail swamp.

In a roadside thicket we are likely to see the cuckoos, both the yellow-billed and the black-billed and will most likely find them engaged in nest building. We might also hear in a roadside thicket, if we listen carefully, the brown thrasher scratching among the dead leaves, but the chances of seeing the bird are rather remote as he is rather shy and furtive and apt to retire into the underbrush; we see him more often when he calls to his mate in loud clear tones from some sapling. And if we are lucky, we might also see in some shaded thicket along the roadside the redstart, whirling and dashing like a flaming will-o'-the-wisp, and perhaps hear the plaintive "pee-wee" of the wood pewee hidden on a leafy branch of some nearby tree.

In the tangled underbrush of a wet, bushy meadow or of a swampy thicket we might hear the yellowthroat, easily recognized by the male's black mask, nervously voicing his alarm at our presence with scolding chirps and chattering notes. And in such places, as a brush-grown fence, a hedgerow, a roadside thicket, and the edge of a swamp, we can invariably find the yellow warbler, also known as the wild canary, cavorting like an animated sunbeam; we might even see him in our garden on occasion.

On almost any day we can glimpse the scarlet tanager flashing red against the azure sky or among the countless apple blossoms, resplendent in the sunshine, or a northern (Baltimore) oriole weaving his way, singing his song of joy, or perhaps we will hear from a field of daisies, buttercups, and clovers the music of the bobolink bubbling up in a cascade of ecstasy.

The vireos, the red-eyed, warbling, and yellow throated, are essentially birds of the woodlands, but they may also nest in orchards and in shade trees along the streets of towns and villages; I have often seen the red-eyed building her dainty, handsome little basket in the crotch of an apple tree. The wood thrush is truly a bird of the woods, and we can often hear him tuning his lyre amid the misty greenery of a shady nook. At times we can see the ovenbird walking along the woodland floor like a diminutive chicken, and sometimes we might come across the towhee scratching among the leaves of a clearing in the manner of a fox sparrow. Should we come upon a woodland glade through which a brook flows on its way to the sea and where sunbeams dance upon the water that dimples over moss-grown rocks and fallen logs, we might see the water thrush walking in the water or teetering up and down on a log while wagging his tail in the usual thrushlike manner. And at night the loud, clear notes of the whippoorwill echo through the woods.

The swallows are much in evidence—the bank, the cliff, and the barn—and through the years the barn swallow has invariably built its nest in my garage. The purple martin, too, is a familiar summer visitor as is also the chimney swift; in the twilight of the evening we can see the swifts, with quivering wings and shrill twitterings, describe a lacework of disappearing lines against the sky as they pursue flying insects. And almost everywhere—in the orchard, along the roadside, by a fencerow, in the woodland border, in the vicinity of a farm—we can watch the kingbird chase flying insects or, savage and fearless, assailing any bird that gets in his way or interferes with his own welfare, even attacking a hawk or crow with impunity. And more often than not we can spy a number of indigo buntings perched on a telephone wire.

Like the kingbird, which is a flycatcher, both the crested flycatcher and the least flycatcher may often be seen in an orchard, though both may also be found in the woods. The house wren and catbird are also attracted to the orchard, but both of them may be seen in our gardens; indeed, the house wren may occupy a birdhouse if one is available, and the catbird has often nested in the lilacs about my house.

Wood ducks are a familiar sight on almost any pond, and invariably the spotted sandpiper is too; the green heron may also be seen quite frequently in the vicinity of the water. And how often have I seen a kingfisher suddenly leave his perch in a tree to fly above the water, then quickly dive into it to return a moment later with a fish in his bill!

Afterword

It is a truism that everything that has a beginning must have an end; because this book had a beginning it must, unfortunately, have an end. I say "unfortunately" because I enjoyed writing *Suburban Wildlife*—it brought back memories of seventy years of exploring and following the bypaths of nature.

I say "seventy years" because I was a boy of about ten years of age when I wrote my first book; I use the word "book" advisedly because it was merely a dime store copy book in which I pasted pictures of birds that came with packets of cigarettes that my father collected from the men where he worked. I remember copying a brief account of each bird from the reverse side of the card, and putting my notes into the book. I also worked as time permitted in getting together an insect collection, and like other small boys had a menagerie of sorts: a rabbit, a field mouse, a snake. All of these hobbies were later to give a direction to my life.

It is tragic to think that even in these ecologically-conscious times many of us live out the Great Adventure without knowing much about the world in which we live. There are some people I know who can't tell the difference between a chipmunk and a squirrel, or a robin and a bluebird, or a dandelion and an aster. These are extreme cases to be sure, but they make my point. And perhaps it doesn't matter in our struggle for survival and in our mad pursuit of the almighty dollar. But I want to think that there is something more to life; after all, we are all an integral part of our environment, and it should be to our advantage to know something of the world in which we live—if for no other reason than for our own enlightenment and well-being, and for the enjoyment of the beauties that are all around us, but to which most of us are blind.

There is a thrill in hearing the chipping of the chipping sparrow, in hearing the melodious notes of the wood thrush, in catching a glimpse of red against the blue sky, in noting that the scarlet tanager is on the wing, in watching the chimney swifts describe disappearing lines in the evening sky, in suddenly being startled by hearing the bass notes of the bullfrog break the quiet of a summer's evening; in watching a butterfly with shimmering wings fly erratically over a field of daisies and buttercups, stopping here and there for a sip of nectar, in spying a chipmunk suddenly appear on a stone wall and look at you with inquisitive eyes, or in pausing and contemplating the beauty of a wildflower and marvelling at how delicately and ingeniously it is put

lives and in their adjustments we might also find
problems.

so the present book came into being, with the purpose
an interest in the wildlife about us, in all the various kinds
that we find along the roadside, in the fields and woods, in
s and streams, and in our own back yards and gardens. I hope
his book has provided the reader with a new perspective into the
rld in which we live, and that it has expanded the reader's awareness
of the enjoyment and richness of life that can be gained by becoming
better acquainted with Nature. It is with this thought that the author
takes leave of his readers.